Gluten-Free Without Rice

Easy Cooking for
Variety on a
Gluten-Free Diet

Nicolette M. Dumke

GLUTEN-FREE WITHOUT RICE:
EASY COOKING FOR VARIETY
ON A GLUTEN-FREE DIET

Published by
Adapt Books
Allergy Adapt, Inc.
1877 Polk Avenue
Louisville, Colorado 80027
303-666-8253

ISBN 10: 1-887624-15-5
ISBN 13: 978-1-887624-15-2
LCCN: 2007903332

Dedication

To my Sweetie Pies –
my sons Joel and John

To have spent my life
loving and being loved by
you is the greatest blessing
anyone can have.

I am so proud of the way
you deal with the
challenges of higher education
and responsibilities
of adult life.

I love you with all my heart.

Love,
Mom

Disclaimer

The information contained in this book is merely intended to communicate food preparation material and information about possible treatment options which are helpful and educational to the reader. It is not intended to replace medical diagnosis or treatment, but rather to provide information and recipes which may be helpful in implementing a diet prescribed by your doctor. Please consult your physician for medical advice before embarking on any treatment or changing your diet.

The author and publisher declare that to the best of their knowledge all material in this book is accurate; however, although unknown to the author and publisher, some recipes may contain ingredients which may be harmful to some people.

There are no warranties which extend beyond the educational nature of this book, either expressed or implied, including, but not limited to, the implied warranties of merchantability, fitness for a particular purpose, or non-infringement. Therefore, the author and publisher shall have neither liability nor responsibility to any person with respect to any loss or damage alleged to be caused, directly or indirectly, by the information contained in this book.

If you do not wish to be bound by the above, you may return this book to the publisher for a full refund.

Table of Contents

About This Book's Cover

The goodies on this book's cover were made from recipes in this book. Clockwise from the top right they are:

Carrot Cookies, page 71, made with quinoa
Chocolate Brownies, page 65, made with buckwheat
"Graham" Crackers, page 34, made with quinoa
Cornbread, page 38
Buckwheat Waffles, page 27
Almond Waffles, page 26, made with arrowroot
Center – Amaranth Blueberry Muffins, page 32

Acknowledgements

Cover photography was done by Joel Dumke and we had a wonderful time doing it. Thanks for the photo and the memories, Sweetie!

Cover design was done by Ed Nies, Mel Typesetting, 1523 S. Pearl Street, Suite B, Denver, CO 80210.

Special thanks go to the greatest editor and cheerleader around, Joan Hinkemeyer, Editorial Services, 2465 S. Humboldt Street, Denver, CO 80210. She not only edited this book; she also advised and encouraged me as I was writing it. She is gluten-intolerant and also tasted many of the recipes.

Finally, special thanks to my many other tasters: John Dumke, Mark Dumke, Joel Dumke, Gina Jiannetti-Wellington, Connie Tysdal, Athena Eliopulos, and numerous other friends.

Cooking for a Gluten-Free Diet

The amount of cooking that a gluten-free diet – or any special diet – requires can seem overwhelming. However, with knowledge, organization, experience and the use of some modern kitchen appliances, the task will become easier. As your health improves, you will have more energy and may find that, even with additional cooking, you are able to do more things and experience more enjoyment in life.

KNOWLEDGE

The saying, "Knowledge is power," applies to a gluten-free diet. If you have not cooked "from scratch" before, the first step to cooking easily for your diet is to learn more about cooking. For the basics of cooking, see *Easy Cooking for Special Diets* as described on the last pages of this book.

For a gluten-free diet, knowledge is also economy. Cooking for yourself or your family member not only adds variety to what you eat, it also saves money. At the time of this writing, a small loaf of rice bread or rice-containing tapioca bread costs $5.69 at my store. By using the recipes in this book, you can eat your fill of baked goods made with a different grain every day for less than you would spend on this bread.

The most crucial thing you need to know when cooking for a gluten-free diet is how to bake. Because it is more difficult to get gluten-free baked goods to rise well, baking with gluten-free flours is more exacting than baking with wheat flour. Even experienced cooks will need to pay more attention to baking technique. Be sure to measure accurately. Because cooking with gluten-free flours is more exacting than cooking with wheat, you will find measurements used in this book that are not used often in "normal" cooking, such as $\frac{3}{8}$ cup, $\frac{1}{8}$ teaspoon, etc. For more about how to "read" these amounts on your measuring cups and spoons and for more information about measuring accurately in general, see "About Measurements" on pages 85 to 86.

The procedure which should be followed when making baking-powder leavened baked goods (muffins, quick breads, cookies, pancakes, cakes, etc.) with gluten-free flours is as follows: Preheat your oven to the temperature specified in the recipe. Oil your baking sheets or oil and flour your pan or muffin cups using the same flour you are using in the recipe. It is important to do these things first so you do not have to spend time doing them after your dough or batter is mixed.

Stir the dry ingredients together in a large bowl. Mix the liquid ingredients in another bowl or in the cup you used to measure them. Before the oil and water or other liquids can separate, quickly stir them into the dry ingredients until they are just mixed. It is better to undermix than overmix. If you undermix, the floury spots will probably moisten up in baking. If you overmix, you will "use up" the leavening power of the baking powder during mixing rather than having this power act in the oven where the leavening should cause your muffins, bread, etc. to rise.

As soon as the ingredients are mixed, quickly put the batter into the prepared pan and slide it into the preheated oven. Bake for the shortest time specified in the recipe. Then look at it. Is it beginning to brown? Is bread beginning to pull away from the sides of the pans slightly? If you think your muffins, cake or bread might be done, stick a toothpick into the center. If the toothpick comes out dry, it is done. If there is moist batter (not dry crumbs) on the toothpick, bake for another five to ten minutes and then test with a toothpick again.

Most of the recipes in this book instruct you to remove your baked goods from the pan immediately. A few recipes, such as the cake recipes, will tell you to cool your cake in the pan for a short time before removing it or to serve it from the pan. If you are leaving a cake in the pan, put the pan on a cooling rack when you take it from the oven. After you remove bread or cakes from the pan, also put them on a cooling rack and cool them completely before slicing the bread or frosting the cake. Muffins, crackers, and cookies you can enjoy hot from the oven! Any muffins that you don't eat right away should be cooled on a rack. Cool cookies and crackers on paper towels. After your baked goods are cool, store them in plastic bags or containers to help them retain moisture.

ORGANIZATION

Organization also makes cooking for a special diet, or any diet, much easier. Stock your kitchen with the ingredients you need for a gluten-free diet. As described in the next chapter, these items include a variety of gluten-free grains, flours and starches, leavenings such as baking powder and yeast, healthy sweeteners and oils, and special ingredients that will help your baked goods rise, such as guar gum or xanthum gum and eggs.

Organize your time as well as your kitchen. Grocery shop once a week using a list. If you notice that you are running low on a certain staple flour or other ingredient between shopping trips, put it on your grocery list so that you can replenish your supply before you actually run out of the ingredient. This saves time on emergency trips to the grocery store or health food store in the middle of a baking session!

Make use of your freezer. Prepare large batches of baked goods and main dishes and freeze them for future use. This is possible even if the only freezer you have is the small one at the top of your refrigerator. Do not store more than one week's supply of frozen vegetables, juices, and other easily purchased foods in the freezer section of your refrigerator; save most of the space for your specially prepared foods. Freeze serving-sized portions of main dishes in Ziploc™ storage bags so they take up less room than if frozen in assorted size plastic containers and will "pack" into your freezer efficiently. Invest in a few square or rectangular Tupperware™ (or similar) containers of uniform size for freezing cookies, crackers and other fragile baked goods. Try to keep your freezer organized (for example, assign breads a certain location in the freezer) so you can find the food you are looking for quickly. If you are hungry, it can be very frustrating not to be able to find what you need to eat!

TIME-SAVING APPLIANCES

Take advantage of time-saving appliances. A hand blender will make homemade gravies and sauces easy to make lump-free as well as helping you make "Almond Waffles," page 26. A crock pot can have your dinner ready for you to eat when you arrive home from work or from driving the kids to after-school activities. See *Allergy Cooking with Ease* or *The Ultimate Food Allergy Cookbook and Survival Guide* for recipes for gluten-free main dishes, soups, and stews made with a crock pot. If you want to eat yeast bread often, a bread machine can be a lifesaver. See *Easy Breadmaking for Special Diets* for information on how to choose the machine that will best meet your needs. All of these books are described on the last pages of this book.

If you have an oven with a time-bake feature, will be at home, or will be gone for only an hour or so before dinnertime, an "oven meal" can simplify your life. Put a roast, ham, or chicken in the oven along with any of the oven vegetables and oven grains on pages 45 to 50 and a dessert such as "Easy Fruit Tapioca" or baked apples or pears (page 64). In an hour or two, dinner will be ready, and you can be doing whatever you need to do during that time. For more about oven meals including menus, see *Easy Cooking for Special Diets*.

A FINAL WORD

Be patient with yourself. Cooking for a special diet takes some getting used to. As you gain experience, it will become easier. Making the effort to cook for yourself or your family member(s) is very much worth it. As your health improves, all of life will become easier and more enjoyable. You can do it! Go for it!

Know Your Ingredients

The difference between gluten-free cooking and "regular" cooking is – obviously – that we use only gluten-free foods and ingredients. On a gluten-free diet you will come to know these foods and ingredients intimately and will realize that although gluten-free flours behave much differently than wheat (precisely because they are gluten-free) they are delicious and produce wonderful foods.

TRUE GRAINS

Several of the flours which can be used on a gluten-free diet are botanically classified as members of the grain family and therefore are true grains. Rice is a member of the grain family, as is wild rice. All of the gluten-free grains are more crumbly than wheat in baked goods but have good flavor. The true grains used in the recipes in this book are:

CORN is a very pleasant tasting gluten-free grain. Cornmeal is widely available in grocery stores and adds an interesting texture to baked goods. You can get corn flour, which is similar to cornmeal but is ground to a smoother texture, at your health food store.

TEFF has been difficult to find in the past, but now Bob's Red Mill™ has made it easily available. If your health food store does not carry it, it is likely that they do carry some of Bob's other products and can easily get it in for you. Teff is a little less bland than the other gluten-free grains but is still delicious. Teff flour tends to be a little gritty but makes very nice baked products.

MILLET is quite crumbly and tends to produce very dry baked goods no matter how much oil or pureed fruit you use in the recipe. However, it has an excellent flavor. Whole millet is delicious as "Millet Mashed Potatoes," page 50, and is very easy to cook in the oven. (See the recipe on page 45). Millet and millet flour are usually available at health food stores. However, if your store doesn't carry them, you or your store can order them. For ordering information, see "Sources," page 80.

SORGHUM, which is also called **MILO** or **JOWAR**, is a sweet and delicious non-gluten grain. Like millet, it tends to produce dry baked goods. It is often used to make sorghum molasses and has traditionally been fed to cattle. It used to be difficult to find but now is produced by Bob's Red Mill™. If your health food store does not carry it, ask them to get it in for you. For ordering information, see "Sources," pages 80 and 82.

OATS have recently been allowed on gluten-free diets by some doctors. They do contain a low level of gluten-like proteins, so it is possible that not all celiacs will tolerate them. Oats are delicious and have a familiar flavor, but an occasional batch of oat flour may produce gummy baked goods.

NON-GRAINS

The non-grains are not botanically related to wheat. Many of them are the seeds of the plants that they grow on, so they are very nutritious and high in protein. In the recipes in this book, the seed flours are often used with small quantities of a starch to help them stick together. The non-grains include:

AMARANTH is in the same botanical order as quinoa, although it is not in the same food family. Because it is not a grain, it is a welcome dietary addition for those allergic to all grains. It makes very tasty baked goods. Purchase it at a store that refrigerates its flour and refrigerate or freeze it at home since it may develop an unpleasantly strong flavor if stored too long at room temperature. An occasional batch of amaranth flour will yield gummy pancakes or bread, but the recipes included in this book (crackers, muffins, cookies) rarely have this problem.

QUINOA boasts a high content of high-quality protein. It is one of the best protein sources, due to its amino acid balance, among plant foods. For this reason, it is very satisfying to eat; quinoa baked goods really "stick with you." Those allergic to all grains will find quinoa a welcome dietary staple. It has a distinctive taste so goes well with other strongly flavored ingredients such as cinnamon, sesame seeds and carob. Quinoa flour is excellent in baked goods of all kinds and makes good yeast bread. Whole grain quinoa has a natural soapy coating on it, so before you cook it, put it in a strainer and rinse it under running water until the water is no longer sudsy. This coating protects the plant from insects. Quinoa is in the same food family as spinach, beets, and Swiss chard.

BUCKWHEAT is a very versatile non-grain flour. It is excellent in waffles and pancakes, and a chocolate-eating celiac friend raves about "Chocolate Brownies," page 65, made with buckwheat flour. In a few recipes (such crackers and muffins, which are not included in this book) it can have a strong flavor. It is in the same food family as rhubarb.

BEAN FLOURS such as **GARBANZO, GARFAVA,** and **FAVA FLOUR** are also high protein additions to the gluten-free diet. They do not stick together well and must be used with larger quantities of other flours or starches.

CAROB POWDER is also a bean flour since carob beans are in the legume family. However, it is usually used as a chocolate substitute rather than as the main ingredient of baked goods. Carob chips are a welcome addition to cookies for those who are allergic to chocolate.

NUT MEALS such as almond meal and hazelnut meal are great additions to baked goods. You can make delicious crunchy waffles from almond meal and a starch. See the recipe on page 26.

There are several white, highly refined starches that are commonly used in gluten-free cooking. They include **ARROWROOT, TAPIOCA FLOUR/STARCH, WATER CHESTNUT STARCH, CORNSTARCH,** and **BEAN STARCH.** These starches serve as binders in gluten-free baking and can also be used as thickeners for sauces and gravies. Arrowroot and tapioca starch can be substituted for each other in baking in equal quantities. Sauces thickened with tapioca tend to be a little more ropy than those thickened with arrowroot, and you made need slightly more tapioca than arrowroot.

POTATO FLOUR and **POTATO STARCH** (also called potato starch flour) may also be used in gluten-free cooking. They are not the same thing, however, and cannot be used interchangeably. Potato flour is made from whole potatoes and retains the nutritional value of potatoes including considerable protein. In baking, it must be used with eggs (usually it is folded into beaten egg whites) or the baked product may end up like mashed potatoes on the inside. Potato starch is a highly refined starch, much like the starches in the preceding paragraph, except that it attracts and holds moisture, or is hygroscopic. Both of these ingredients must be used in small amounts in most recipes or their hygroscopic nature may cause a gooey texture in the final product.

"Exotic" flours such as **CHESTNUT FLOUR, CASSAVA MEAL,** and **TUBER FLOURS** are useful for individuals sensitive to all grains. Cassava meal can be used for breading meat and fish and for crackers and is not too expensive. Chestnut flour and flours made from a variety of unusual tubers may be needed by those with extremely extensive food allergies but they are expensive. For recipes made with these flours, see *The Ultimate Food Allergy Cookbook and Survival Guide* which is described on the last pages of this book.

There is now a rice-free **BAKING MIXTURE** composed of several flours which is produced by Bob's Red Mill™. It contains garbanzo bean flour, potato starch, tapioca starch, white sorghum flour, and fava bean flour and is called Bob's Red Mill™ Gluten-Free All Purpose Baking Flour. Recipes using this mix are available on the Bob's Red Mill™ website.

LEAVENINGS AND BINDERS

Leavenings are the ingredients that make baked products rise. They include baking powder, baking soda combined with an acid ingredient, and yeast. Binders help the leavenings "work" by trapping the gas the leavenings produce. Binders are not needed when you bake with wheat because the gluten in wheat flour forms sheets that trap the gas. They include eggs, starches (discussed on pages 15 and 16), and fibers such as guar gum and xanthum gum.

BAKING POWDER is a combination of acid and basic components that, when moistened, produces gas to make baked goods rise in baking. Some brands of baking powder contain aluminum, which should probably be avoided for best health. Bob's Red Mill™ produces a good aluminum-free baking powder which is sold in large economical bags. I store my Bob's™ baking powder in small jars to keep it "dry and potent" until I finish using the whole bag. Most commercial baking powder contains cornstarch. If you are sensitive to corn, use Featherweight™ baking powder which contains potato starch instead.

BAKING SODA is pure sodium bicarbonate and is almost universally tolerated by people with severe food allergies. For those on rotation diets, it is usually allowed every day of the rotation cycle. It must be used in conjunction with an acid ingredient to make baked goods rise. The acid ingredients commonly used include buttermilk, lemon juice or other fruit juices, and cream of tartar. For the very allergic, unbuffered vitamin C crystals are the best way to provide the acid component of the leavening process. Therefore, most of the recipes in *The Ultimate Food Allergy Cookbook and Survival Guide* and *Allergy Cooking with Ease* contain a built-in baking powder made of baking soda and unbuffered vitamin C crystals.

BAKER'S YEAST is what makes commercial bread rise and is available in many forms. Active dry yeast is yeast that has been freeze-dried to retain its activity. An expiration date is usually stamped on the package and the yeast should be good until that date if you store it in the refrigerator after opening it. Active dry yeast is available in ¼ ounce (2¼ teaspoon) packets or 4 ounce jars in most grocery stores. In addition, you can purchase it in 1 pound bags and store the yeast in your freezer. Do not thaw and refreeze this yeast; instead occasionally take out a small amount to use within a few weeks and keep it in a jar in the refrigerator. Leave the remainder of the yeast frozen. Red Star™ active dry yeast is free of gluten and preservatives and works well in bread machines as well as in the recipes in this book. Instant or quick-rise yeasts leaven bread more rapidly than active dry yeast. They are useful for making bread more quickly. These "fast" types of yeast are not recommended for gluten-free breads because their structure is more fragile. If quick-rise yeasts are used, the bread may over-rise and then collapse during baking.

EGGS and **FRUIT PUREES** are binders that are also used in "normal" baking. These ingredients help your baked goods hold together while adding nutritional value and flavor.

GUAR GUM and **XANTHUM GUM** are two types of soluble fiber used as binders in gluten-free baking. They both can be fairly allergenic, so I use them only in yeast breads where they are actually essential. If you have problems with one of them, you can substitute the other in the same amount in recipes. Guar gum is made from a legume. Xanthum gum is derived from a type of bacteria, *Xanthomonas compestris*.

SWEETENERS

Most of the recipes in this book are sweetened with fruit sweeteners or honey rather than sugar. Fruit sweeteners contain fructose, a simple sugar which can be directly absorbed without any digestion and does not cause wide swings in blood sugar levels like refined sugar (sucrose) does. Although honey may contribute more to blood sugar problems, it is not highly refined and still contains many minerals and other nutrients.

LIQUID FRUIT SWEETENERS make delicious and healthy baked goods. The least concentrated of these are pureed fruits and fruit juice concentrates. Apple juice concentrate is used in many of the recipes in this book. I routinely keep a can of frozen concentrate in my refrigerator so I'm ready to bake at all times. More concentrated liquid fruit sweeteners include Fruit Sweet™ which is a blend of peach, pear, and pineapple juices, Pear Sweet™ and Grape Sweet™. Using these sweeteners, you can make desserts so similar to sugar-containing desserts that no one will know they do not contain sugar. They are used in only a few recipes in this book because most smaller health food stores do not carry them, but they can be ordered easily and make such good desserts that they are very much worth ordering. See "Sources," page 83 for information about ordering these sweeteners from Wax Orchards.

DATE SUGAR is ground dried dates. It is a concentrated sweetener which is very useful in desserts where more sweetness is desired. It also helps keep your baked goods moist. It is the only dry sweetener used in this book aside from a few recipes for chocolate cookies and cakes sweetened with sugar.

HONEY and **MOLASSES** are less refined sweeteners that add moistness and flavor to baked goods. Honey is used in recipes in this book where more sweetness is desired than can be achieved with fruit juice concentrates. Molasses is used in the gingerbread recipe. Although they are potent sweeteners which may have more effect on blood sugar levels than fruit sweeteners, unlike white sugar, they have not been stripped of their content of minerals and other nutrients.

RICE SYRUP is another sweetener which may be allowed on gluten-free diets if it is made without barley or other grains. Because this book avoids rice, it is not used in these recipes. It is less sweet than fruit sweeteners. Baked products made with rice syrup do not brown as much as those made with other sweeteners.

SUGAR is an ingredient which I normally avoid using in cooking. It has been stripped of the nutrients naturally present in sugar cane or sugar beets and can have a profound effect on blood sugar levels and intestinal flora. However, it is used in a few chocolate-containing recipes in this book because it was not possible to make them taste "normal" any other way. Please save these sugar-containing recipes for special treats rather than for everyday use.

OTHER INGREDIENTS

The recipes in this book contain a wide variety of other common ingredients. Salt is essential in yeast bread recipes because it moderates the growth of the yeast but can be omitted from any of the other recipes if desired. Most of the recipes in this book are made with oil because it is the healthiest type of fat for us to consume. For further information on fats and oils as well as the more common ingredients used in this book, see *Easy Cooking for Special Diets* as described on the last pages of this book.

The ingredient lists for the recipes in this book are, in most cases, shorter than in some gluten-free recipes books. This makes it take less time to make a recipe. In addition, when the ingredient list contains only those items which are absolutely necessary, those with food allergies are more likely to be able to use the recipe without leaving something out or making a substitution.

INGREDIENT SUBSTITIONS

When you bake for a gluten free diet, you will need to purchase many "new" ingredients. You may often wonder if you can substitute something else for that new ingredient you do not have on hand! Substitutions are tricky in gluten-free baking. The recipes in this book should work as written (although an unusual batch of flour from a health food store bulk bin can upset any recipe), but if you substitute, there are no guarantees.

People call me and say, "I've got your recipe made with quinoa flour and I want to make it with oat flour. How can I do this?" I usually can't give them a definite answer, although I try to make suggestions that may or may not work. In my experience, there is no "rule" or conversion factor for substitutions between any two types of flour that works predictably.

The "bottom line" on flour substitutions is this: be prepared to tweak a recipe made with a substitute flour several times before it is right or even to never have it work. If there is not a recipe for something you want in this book, see *The Ultimate Food Allergy Cookbook and Survival Guide* as described on the last pages of this book. Because that book is designed to be the "ultimate" help for people whose diets may be extremely limited, I attempted to make each type of flour (including rarely eaten foods such as tuber flours, chestnut flour, starch flours, and non-gluten grain flours) into as many types of recipes as possible and only omitted a certain recipe if it really was not possible to make. For example, the only reason the book does not contain a recipe for sorghum yeast bread is because I was unable, after many tries, to make a loaf that did not collapse. However, it does have a sorghum non-yeast bread recipe made with eggs to help hold it together. (This is one of the very few egg-containing recipes in the book). There are also recipes for fruited sorghum non-yeast bread (where the fiber in the fruit keeps it together) and sorghum muffins, crackers, tortillas, pancakes, cake, and cookies. As mentioned earlier in this chapter, buckwheat can be bitter in crackers and muffins, so these recipes were not included in *Gluten-Free Without Rice*. However, since there are severely allergic people who can eat only one or two grain alternatives, the recipes for buckwheat crackers and muffins are in *The Ultimate Food Allergy Cookbook and Survival Guide*.

Unlike wheat flour, milk is an ingredient where substitutions in "normal" recipes usually work. In most recipes, you can replace the milk called for with an equal amount of water. Sometimes you can replace milk with fruit juice, but the acidity of the juice can affect the leavening process and result in a collapse of your baked product. Gluten-free yeast breads, in which the protein content contributed by the milk helps strengthen the structure of the bread, can be an exception to the "rule" that water can be substituted for milk.

In allergy baking, eggs can usually be replaced with an equal volume of water if the recipe is not depending on the egg for structure. However, in a recipe made with a gluten-free or low gluten flour, the egg sometimes is serving to replace part of the structure normally provided by gluten, and replacing the egg with water may lead to a collapse.

Home ground flour may also behave differently than commercially ground flour, and it can vary from batch to batch of grain. If you use either very finely milled flour or coarsely milled or blender-ground flour you will have to change the amount of liquid used in the recipe. Unless you are willing to experiment with each new batch of grain when you grind your own flour, it is best to purchase flour from a reliable commercial source.

Breakfast Foods

What's for breakfast? Eggs are gluten-free, but eggs every day might be a bit much for your cholesterol! Also, for those with food allergies, eggs are often a problem food. The breakfast foods in this chapter are made with gluten-free grains and are a great alternative to eggs. These delicious pancakes and waffles freeze well and are tasty reheated. The waffles may be reheated in your toaster and pancakes can be microwaved or heated in a toaster oven. The granola recipes at the end of the chapter give you a breakfast cereal that is ready to eat but unlike many commercial cereals does not contain sugar and unhealthy fats. For more delicious breakfast foods, see the muffin and bread recipes in the next chapter.

Buckwheat Pancakes

These pancakes are light and fluffy. Any leftovers are great reheated.

> 2 cups buckwheat flour
> 3 teaspoons baking powder
> ½ teaspoon salt
> 2 tablespoons oil
> 2½ cups water or apple juice OR 2 cups of water plus
>   ½ cup apple juice concentrate

Lightly oil a pancake griddle and heat it over medium heat. If you are using an electric griddle, heat it to 350°F. Mix together the flour, baking powder, and salt. Combine the oil with the water and/or juice and stir them into the flour mixture with a wire whisk to make a thin batter. Pour ⅛ to ¼ cup of batter onto the griddle for each pancake. The batter may thicken as you are cooking the pancakes. If your pancakes start coming out too thick, add water to the batter 1 tablespoon at a time to return it to the right consistency. Cook the pancakes until they are dry on the top and light brown on the bottom, then turn and cook them until the second side is light brown. Makes about 2 dozen 3-inch pancakes or 1½ dozen 4-inch pancakes.

Corn Pancakes

The cornmeal gives these pancakes a delightful texture. They are especially delicious with peach jam.

⅓ cup corn meal
⅓ cup boiling water
½ cup corn flour
1 teaspoon baking powder
¼ teaspoon salt
1 tablespoon honey
2 tablespoons oil
⅔ cup cold milk or cold water
1 large egg

Lightly oil your pancake griddle and heat it over medium heat. If you are using an electric griddle, heat it to 350°F. In a medium-sized bowl, stir together the corn meal and boiling water. Let them cool while you measure the corn flour, baking powder, and salt into another bowl. Then add the honey and oil to the wet cornmeal and stir. Lightly beat the egg with a fork. Add the cold milk or water and egg to the cornmeal mixture and stir until smooth and all the lumps of cornmeal are broken up. Stir together the dry ingredients in the second bowl. Then add the cornmeal mixture to the dry ingredients and stir until just mixed. Pour ⅛ to ¼ cup of batter onto the griddle for each pancake. Cook the pancakes until the whole top surface of each pancake looks dull and the bottom is brown. Then turn and cook the second side until it begins to brown. Makes about one dozen 3 to 4 inch pancakes.

Sorghum Pancakes

2¼ cups sorghum (milo) flour
1 cup arrowroot
3 teaspoons baking powder
½ teaspoon salt
¼ cup oil
1¾ cups water or apple juice OR 1¼ cups water plus
    ½ cup apple juice concentrate

Lightly oil a pancake griddle and heat it over medium heat. If you are using an electric griddle, heat it to 350°F. Mix together the flour, arrowroot, baking powder, and salt. Combine the oil with the water and/or juice and stir them into the flour mixture with a wire whisk to make a thin batter. Pour ⅛ to ¼ cup of batter onto the griddle for each pancake. If the batter thickens while you are cooking the pancakes, add an extra 2 to 6 tablespoons of water to the batter one tablespoon at a time to return it to the right consistency. Cook the pancakes until they are dry on the top and light brown on the bottom, then turn and cook them until the second side is light brown. Makes about 2 dozen 3-inch pancakes or 1½ dozen 4-inch pancakes.

Teff Pancakes

These pancakes got mixed reviews from a few of my tasters, but if you like the flavor of teff, you'll enjoy them.

2 cups teff flour
3 teaspoons baking powder
½ teaspoon salt
2 tablespoons oil
2 cups water or apple juice OR 1½ cups of water
    plus ½ cup apple juice concentrate

Lightly oil a pancake griddle and heat it over medium heat. If you are using an electric griddle, heat it to 350°F. Mix together the flour, baking powder, and salt. Combine the oil with the water and/or juice and stir them into the flour mixture with a wire whisk to make a thin batter. Pour ⅛ to ¼ cup of batter onto the griddle for each pancake. If the batter thickens while you are cooking the pancakes, add an extra 2 to 4 tablespoons of water to the batter one tablespoon at a time to return it to the right consistency. Cook the pancakes until they are dry on the top and light brown on the bottom, then turn and cook them until the second side is light brown. Makes about 2 dozen 3-inch pancakes or 1½ dozen 4-inch pancakes.

Quinoa Pancakes

1½ cups quinoa flour
½ cup tapioca starch
3 teaspoons baking powder
1½ teaspoons cinnamon
3 tablespoons oil
2 cups water or apple juice OR 1½ cups water plus
    ½ cup apple juice concentrate, thawed

Lightly oil a pancake griddle and heat it over medium heat. If you are using an electric griddle, heat it to 350°F. Mix together the flour, starch, baking powder, and cinnamon. Combine the oil with the water and/or juice and stir them into the flour mixture with a wire whisk to make a thin batter. Pour ⅛ to ¼ cup of batter onto the griddle for each pancake. If the first batch of pancakes you cook is too thick, add an extra 2 to 4 tablespoons of water to the batter one tablespoon at a time to return it to the right consistency. Cook the pancakes until they are dry on the top and light brown on the bottom, then turn and cook them until the second side is light brown. Makes about 2 dozen 3-inch pancakes or 1½ dozen 4-inch pancakes.

Almond Waffles

These crunchy waffles are great for snacks.

1⅜ cups almond meal/flour
1¾ cups arrowroot or tapioca starch
⅛ teaspoon salt
1¾ cups water
1 tablespoon oil

Brush your waffle iron with oil. Heat the iron on "high" for 15 minutes before you begin cooking waffles. (If the iron is not hot enough, you may have difficulty removing the waffles from the iron). While the iron is heating, measure the ingredients and mix the batter. First, stir the almond meal before measuring it because it tends to become packed together in the bag. Measure the almond meal, starch, and salt into a deep mixing bowl or 4-cup measuring cup if you will be using a hand blender or into the bowl of a blender or food processor with the "puree" blade in place. Add the water and oil. Blend with a hand blender, food processor or blender. If you have time, let the batter stand 5 minutes before beginning to cook the waffles. Then, for the first waffle and each waffle you make, re-blend right before putting batter in the iron. Put enough batter into the iron for it to reach to about ½ to 1 inch from the edge of the iron (about 1½ cups for a large iron that makes four square waffles). Overfilling the iron may make the waffles difficult to remove. Cook on high for 15 to 18 minutes or until golden brown and crisp. Do not peek into the iron until the waffles should be done and the iron is no longer steaming or you may split the waffles down the middle. Reheat your waffle iron until the light goes off before cooking more waffles. If you do not eat your waffles immediately, cool them on a wire rack. If these waffles soften after they are cool, cook them longer the next time. Makes 8 to 12 4-inch square waffles.

Buckwheat Waffles

These waffles are very light and fluffy and I have received many compliments on them. One of my tasters and good friend Athena Eliopulos said they were great for "savory pairings."

> 2 cups buckwheat flour
> 3 teaspoons baking powder
> ½ teaspoon salt
> ¼ cup oil
> 1¾ cups water

Preheat a lightly oiled waffle iron to medium-high. While the iron is heating, combine the flour, baking powder, and salt in a large bowl. Mix the oil and water, stir them into the dry ingredients, and allow the batter to stand for about 10 minutes while the iron finishes heating. Pour enough batter into the iron to almost reach the edges (about 1 cup for a large iron) and bake for 15 minutes. Do not try to open the iron until each waffle has finished steaming and should be almost done. Makes 12 to 16 4-inch square waffles.

Teff Waffles

> 2½ cups teff flour
> 3 teaspoons baking powder
> ½ teaspoon salt
> ¼ cup oil
> 1¾ cups water

Preheat a lightly oiled waffle iron to medium-high. While the iron is heating, combine the flour, baking powder, and salt in a large bowl. Mix the oil and water, stir them into the dry ingredients, and allow the batter to stand for about 10 minutes while the iron is heating. Pour enough batter into the iron to almost reach the edges (about 1 cup for a large iron) and bake for 15 minutes. Do not try to open the iron until each waffle should be almost done. Makes 12 to 16 4-inch square waffles.

Corn Waffles

2½ cups corn flour
½ teaspoon salt
2 teaspoons baking powder
½ cup oil
1 cup apple juice concentrate, thawed
2 large eggs plus water to bring their volume to ½ cup
¾ cup additional water

Preheat an oiled waffle iron to medium-high. While the iron is heating, combine the flour, baking powder, and salt in a large bowl. Crack the eggs into a measuring cup and lightly beat them with a fork. Add water to the cup to bring the volume up to ½ cup. Then add the apple juice concentrate, additional water, and oil to the eggs. Mix the liquid ingredients thoroughly; then stir them into the dry ingredients. Pour enough batter into the iron to almost reach the edges (about 1 cup for a large iron) and bake for 7 to 10 minutes. Do not try to open the iron until the iron is no longer steaming and the waffle should be almost done. Makes 12 to 16 4-inch square waffles.

Quinoa Granola

This cereal is ready to eat when you are and it is so high in protein that it will sustain you all morning.

1½ cups quinoa flour
½ cup tapioca starch
1½ cups chopped filberts, almonds, or other nuts
½ cup sesame seeds
1½ teaspoons cinnamon
⅓ cup oil
¾ cup unsweetened applesauce
¼ cup apple juice concentrate, thawed
⅔ cup raisins or other dried fruit cut into small pieces

Preheat your oven to 300°F. Lightly oil a 15 inch by 11 inch jelly roll pan, two 13 inch by 9 inch pans, or three cake pans. In a large bowl, stir together the quinoa flour, starch, nuts, sesame seeds, and cinnamon. In a separate bowl or cup, combine the applesauce, apple juice concentrate, and oil. Stir the liquid ingredients into the dry ingredients until they are thoroughly mixed. Spread the granola mixture in the prepared pans and bake for 1 hour to 1 hour and 15 minutes. Stir the granola and break it into chunks with a spoon every 10 to 15 minutes while it is baking. When the granola is golden brown, remove it from the oven and allow it to cool completely in the pan(s). Stir in the dry fruit. Store the granola in airtight containers in a cool place, or freeze it to maintain freshness for long periods of time. Makes 6 to 7 cups of granola.

Amaranth Granola

> 1½ cups amaranth flour
> ½ cup arrowroot or tapioca starch
> 1½ cups chopped walnuts or pecans
> ¼ teaspoon ginger (optional)
> ⅓ cup oil
> ¾ cup mashed bananas
> ¼ cup pineapple juice concentrate, thawed
> ⅔ cup chopped dried bananas, pineapple, or other
>   dried fruit

Preheat your oven to 300°F. Lightly oil a 15 inch by 11 inch jelly roll pan, two 13 inch by 9 inch pans, or three cake pans. In a large bowl, stir together the amaranth flour, starch, nuts, and ginger. In a separate bowl or cup, combine the mashed bananas, pineapple juice concentrate, and oil. Stir the liquid ingredients into the dry ingredients until they are thoroughly mixed. Spread the granola mixture in the prepared pans and bake for 45 to 60 minutes. Stir the granola and break it into chunks with a spoon every 10 to 15 minutes while it is baking. When the granola is golden brown, remove it from the oven and allow it to cool completely in the pan(s). Stir in the dry fruit. Store the granola in airtight containers in a cool place, or freeze it to maintain freshness for long periods of time. Makes 6 to 7 cups of granola.

Oat Granola

Skip the sugar and unhealthy fats you may find in commercial granola cereals! This is traditional granola made with oats for those whose doctors allow them on a gluten-free diet.

> 3 cups rolled oats
> ½ cup oat flour
> ½ cup chopped almonds
> ½ cup sunflower or pumpkin seeds
> ½ cup unsweetened coconut
> ¼ teaspoon ground nutmeg (optional)
> ¼ cup date sugar
> ⅓ cup oil
> ¾ cup pureed peaches, nectarines, or other "juicy" fruit
> ⅔ cup raisins, chopped dates, chopped apricots, or other
>   dried fruit

Preheat your oven to 300°F. Lightly oil a 15 inch by 11 inch jelly roll pan, two 13 inch by 9 inch pans, or three cake pans. In a large bowl, stir together the rolled oats, oat flour, almonds, seeds, coconut, nutmeg, and date sugar. In a separate bowl or cup, combine the pureed fruit and oil. Stir the liquid ingredients into the dry ingredients until they are thoroughly mixed. Spread the granola mixture in the prepared pans and bake for 35 to 45 minutes. Stir the granola every 10 to 15 minutes while it is baking. When the granola is golden brown, remove it from the oven and allow it to cool completely in the pan(s). Stir in the dry fruit. Store the granola in airtight containers in a cool place, or freeze it to maintain freshness for long periods of time. Makes 6 to 7 cups of granola.

Muffins, Crackers and Bread

Daily bread is an important and basic part of our diets and our lives. However, for the gluten-intolerant, especially if you are also rice-intolerant, it may seem hard to find daily bread that you can eat. This chapter contains recipes for muffins, crackers, and breads that will fill the gaps in your diet.

The recipes here are just a sampling of the breads that can be made with non-rice gluten-free flours. If you are allergic to many grains or are on a rotation diet, see *The Ultimate Food Allergy Cookbook and Survival Guide* (described on the last pages of this book) for more recipes made with quinoa, amaranth, buckwheat, teff, sorghum and millet as well as flours not included in this book such as chestnut flour, cassava meal, and tuber flours.

Corn Muffins

2½ cups corn flour
½ teaspoon salt
2 teaspoons baking powder
½ cup oil
1 cup apple juice concentrate, thawed
2 eggs plus water to bring their volume to ½ cup
¼ cup additional water

Preheat your over to 375°F. Line 12 wells of a muffin pan with paper muffin cup liners. Mix the corn flour, salt, and baking powder together in a large bowl. Beat the eggs in a glass measuring cup. Add water to bring the volume in the cup up to ½ cup. Add the apple juice concentrate and oil to the eggs and mix together the liquid ingredients together. Pour the liquid ingredients into the dry ingredients and stir until they are just mixed. Put the batter into the prepared muffin tin, filling each cup about ⅞ full. Bake for 30 to 35 minutes, or until the muffins are brown and a toothpick inserted in the center of a muffin comes out dry. Makes about 12 muffins.

Amaranth Blueberry Muffins

If you are not going to finish eating the whole batch of muffins within a day or so, freeze these muffins to maintain their moistness.

1¾ cups amaranth flour

½ cup arrowroot

3 teaspoons baking powder

¼ teaspoon cinnamon or cloves (optional)

1 large egg*

½ cup plus 1 tablespoon apple juice concentrate, thawed, or enough to bring the total volume of apple juice concentrate plus egg to ¾ cup

¼ cup oil

¾ cup dried blueberries or moist raisins

Preheat your over to 375°F. Line 12 wells of a muffin pan with paper muffin cup liners. Mix the amaranth flour, arrowroot, and baking powder in a large bowl. Stir in the dried fruit. Break the egg into a measuring cup and beat it slightly with a fork. Add apple juice concentrate up to the ¾ cup line. Add the oil to the measuring cup and stir. Pour the liquid ingredients into the dry ingredients and stir until they are just mixed. The batter will be stiffer than for most muffins. Put the batter into the prepared muffin tin filling the cups about ⅞ full. Bake for 15 to 20 minutes or until the muffins brown and a toothpick inserted in the center comes out dry. Makes 10 to 12 muffins.

Note: If you are allergic to eggs or prefer sweeter muffins, substitute ¾ cup apple juice concentrate for the apple juice plus egg.

Sorghum Pineapple Muffins

2 cups sorghum (milo) flour

1 teaspoon baking soda

½ cup pineapple canned in its own juice or fresh pineapple
with juice to cover

1 large egg*

¼ cup + 1 tablespoon pineapple juice concentrate, thawed,
or enough to bring the combined volume of the
pineapple juice concentrate and egg up to ½ cup

⅓ cup oil

Preheat your over to 400°F. Line 12 wells of a muffin pan with paper muffin cup liners. Puree the pineapple in its own juice. (A hand blender works well and can be used to "buzz" together all the liquid ingredients also). Mix the flour and baking soda in a large bowl. Break the egg into a measuring cup and beat slightly with a fork. Add pineapple juice concentrate up to the ½ cup line. Thoroughly mix or hand-blend together the pureed pineapple, pineapple juice concentrate plus egg, and oil. Add the liquid ingredients to the flour mixture and quickly stir and fold together until they are just mixed in. Because the pineapple causes this recipe to "fizz" vigorously, work quickly and do not overmix. Put the batter into the prepared muffin tin filling the cups about ⅞ full. Bake for 15 to 20 minutes or until the muffins begin to brown. Makes about 12 muffins.

Note: If you are allergic to eggs or prefer sweeter muffins, substitute ½ cup pineapple juice concentrate for the pineapple juice concentrate plus egg.

Teff Pineapple Muffins

2 cups teff flour
1 teaspoon baking soda
½ cup pineapple canned in its own juice or fresh pineapple with
    juice to cover
½ cup pineapple juice concentrate, thawed
⅓ cup oil

Preheat your over to 400°F. Line 12 wells of a muffin pan with paper muffin cup liners. Puree the pineapple in its own juice. (A hand blender works well, and can be used to "buzz" together all the liquid ingredients also). Mix the flour and baking soda in a large bowl. Thoroughly mix or hand-blend together the pureed pineapple, pineapple juice concentrate, and oil. Add the liquid ingredients to the flour mixture and quickly stir and fold together until they are just mixed in. Because the pineapple causes this recipe to "fizz" vigorously, work quickly and do not overmix. Put the batter into the prepared muffin tin filling the cups about ⅞ full. Bake for 15 to 20 minutes or until the muffins begin to brown. Makes about 12 muffins.

"Graham" Crackers

3 cups quinoa flour
1 cup tapioca starch
3 teaspoons baking powder
½ teaspoon baking soda
½ teaspoon cinnamon (optional)
1¼ cups apple juice concentrate
½ cup oil

Preheat your oven to 350°F. Oil three baking sheets. Mix together the quinoa flour, tapioca starch, baking powder, and baking soda in a large bowl. Combine the apple juice concentrate and oil and stir them into the dry ingredients until the dough sticks together. Divide the dough into thirds and put each third on to one of the baking sheets.

Flour your rolling pin and the top of the dough. Roll each third to just under ¼ inch thickness. Flour a knife and cut the dough into 1 inch by 3 inch bars. You may have to re-flour the knife between cuts. Prick each bar three times with a fork to resemble graham crackers. Bake for 10 to 15 minutes or until the crackers are lightly browned. Re-cut the crackers on the same lines if necessary. Remove the crackers from the baking sheet using a spatula, and allow them to cool on paper towels. Makes about 3 to 4 dozen crackers.

Sorghum Crackers

1¼ cups sorghum (milo) flour
¾ cup arrowroot
2 teaspoons baking powder
½ teaspoon salt
1 large egg*
Enough additional water to bring the volume of the egg plus
     water up to ½ cup
¼ cup oil

Preheat your oven to 375°F. Lightly oil two baking sheets. Combine the sorghum flour, arrowroot, baking powder, and salt in a large bowl. Beat the egg in a measuring cup. Add water to bring the volume in the cup up to ½ cup. Add the oil to the cup and mix together the liquid ingredients. Add them to the dry ingredients, mixing with your hands to form a stiff dough. Divide the dough in half and roll each part out onto one of the prepared baking sheets with an oiled rolling pin. Cut the dough into 1½ inch squares and bake for 20 to 25 minutes. If the crackers around the edges of the baking sheet are brown before the center, remove them from the baking sheet and allow the crackers in the center to bake longer. Makes about 4 dozen crackers.

Note: If you are allergic to eggs, use ½ cup water instead of the water plus egg.

Teff Crackers

2 cups teff flour
3 teaspoons baking powder
¼ teaspoon salt
½ cup water
¼ cup oil

Preheat your oven to 350°F. Mix together the flour, baking powder, and salt in a large bowl. Combine the water and oil and stir them into the dry ingredients until the dough sticks together. Divide the dough in half. Roll each half to about ⅛ inch thickness on an ungreased baking sheet. Cut the dough into 2 inch squares and sprinkle the tops of the crackers with salt if desired. Bake for 15 to 20 minutes, or until the crackers are crisp and lightly browned. If the crackers around the edges of the baking sheet are brown before the center, remove them from the baking sheet and allow the crackers in the center to bake longer. Makes about 4 dozen crackers.

Quinoa Sesame Seed Crackers

These crackers make a delicious snack that will really satisfy your hunger and stick with you for a long time.

3 cups quinoa flour
1 cup tapioca starch
⅓ cup sesame seeds
5¼ teaspoons baking powder
1 teaspoon salt
1¼ cups water
½ cup oil

Preheat your oven to 350°F. Mix together the quinoa flour, tapioca starch, sesame seeds, baking powder, and salt in a large bowl. Combine the water and oil and stir them into the dry ingredients until the dough comes together. Divide the dough into thirds. Roll each third to about ⅛ inch thickness on an ungreased baking sheet using an oiled rolling pin. If the dough sticks to the rolling pin, lightly flour the top of the dough. After rolling, cut the dough into 2 inch squares and sprinkle the tops of the crackers with salt if desired. Bake for 15 to 25 minutes, or until the crackers are crisp and lightly browned. If the crackers around the edges of the baking sheet are brown before the center, remove them from the baking sheet and allow the crackers in the center to bake longer. Makes about 9 dozen crackers.

Amaranth Crackers

These crackers are so good that I would like to eat them every day.

3 cups amaranth flour
1 cup arrowroot
3 teaspoons baking powder
1 teaspoon salt
¾ cup water
½ cup oil

Preheat your oven to 375°F. Combine the amaranth flour, arrowroot, baking powder, and salt in a large bowl. Mix together the water and oil and pour them into the flour mixture. Stir until the dough sticks together, adding another few tablespoons of water if necessary to form a stiff but not crumbly dough. Divide the dough into thirds. Roll each third to about ⅛ inch thickness on an ungreased baking sheet and cut the dough into 2 inch squares. Sprinkle the tops of the crackers lightly with additional salt if desired. Bake for 15 to 20 minutes, or until the crackers are crisp and lightly browned. If the crackers around the edges of the baking sheet are brown before the center, remove them from the baking sheet and allow the crackers in the center to bake longer. Makes about 9 dozen crackers.

Oat Crackers

These crackers are tasty and easy to make and are included in this book for those who are allowed to eat oats on a gluten-free diet.

> 4 cups quick oats, uncooked
> ½ teaspoon salt
> ⅓ cup oil
> ⅔ cup water

Preheat your oven to 350°F. Lightly oil two baking sheets. Stir the oats and salt together. Add the oil and mix it into the dry ingredients thoroughly. Stir in the water, then mix and knead the dough with your hands until it sticks together. Divide the dough in half; put each half on one of the prepared baking sheets. Lightly rub your rolling pin with oil. Roll the cracker dough out to about ⅛ inch thickness. Cut the dough into 1½ inch squares and sprinkle the crackers lightly with salt. Bake the crackers for 20 to 25 minutes. Watch the crackers closely as the baking time nears completion. If the crackers on the edges of the sheets brown before the baking time is up, remove them from the baking sheet and continue to bake the rest of the crackers. Use a spatula to remove the crackers from the baking sheets when they begin to brown and put them on a paper towel to cool. Makes 3 to 4 dozen crackers.

Cornbread

Making this bread with cornmeal alone gives it an interesting "crunchy" texture.

> ¼ cup honey or Fruit Sweet™
> ¼ cup milk or water
> 2 tablespoons oil
> 2 large eggs, slightly beaten
> 1 cup cornmeal
> ¼ teaspoon salt
> 2 teaspoons baking powder

Preheat your oven to 425°F. Oil an 8 by 4 inch or 9 by 5 inch loaf pan and shake cornmeal around the inside of the pan to coat it well. Stir together the sweetener and milk water until the sweetener is thoroughly "dissolved" and the liquids are well mixed together. Add the oil and eggs and mix well. In a separate bowl, mix together the cornmeal, salt, and baking powder. Stir the liquid into the dry ingredients quickly and pour the batter into the prepared pan. Pop the cornbread into the oven. Bake for 20 to 25 minutes or until it is golden brown and a toothpick inserted in the center of the loaf comes out dry. Cut into squares to serve. Makes 6 to 8 servings.

Sorghum Banana Bread

Although this bread tends to get dry quickly, it has great flavor. Just eat it soon after making it!

> 1⅝ cups sorghum flour
> 1 cup arrowroot or tapioca starch
> ¾ teaspoon salt
> 3 teaspoons baking powder
> 1½ teaspoons cinnamon or ½ teaspoon cloves
> ½ cup chopped nuts (optional)
> 2 large eggs*
> About 1⅜ cups thoroughly mashed ripe bananas
>   (The total volume of mashed bananas plus eggs should
>   be 1¾ cups).
> ¼ cup oil

Preheat your oven to 350°F. Oil and flour an 8 by 4 inch or 9 by 5 inch loaf pan. Stir together the sorghum flour, starch, salt, baking powder, and spice in a large bowl. Mash or puree and measure the bananas. Slightly beat the eggs. Combine the eggs and bananas in a 2-cup measuring cup, adding more bananas if needed to bring the volume up to 1¾ cups. Thoroughly mix the oil into the banana mixture. Add the liquid ingredients to the dry ingredients and stir until they are just mixed. Do not overmix. Quickly scrape the batter into the prepared pan. Put the bread into the oven and bake it for 50 to 60 minutes or until it is brown. Insert a toothpick into the center of the loaf. If it comes out dry, remove the loaf from the oven. Cool the bread in the pan for ten minutes. Then turn the bread out onto a cooling rack and cool it completely before slicing it. If you wish, you can freeze leftover sliced bread. When you want to eat it, toast the slices while still frozen. Makes one loaf of bread.

   ***Note:** If you are allergic to eggs, omit them and use 1¾ cups of mashed bananas.

About Yeast Breads

   Because these recipes were originally developed for people with food allergies, this book takes a different approach to combining several grains in each recipe than many gluten-free cookbooks; most of the recipes in this book are made with a single grain/grain alternative or a single grain/grain alternative plus a starch which acts as a binder. However, when it comes to making yeast breads, a combination of grains plus multiple stabilizers seems to produce bread with a more "normal" texture in most cases. Therefore, only my two best single-grain gluten-free bread recipes are included here. The following recipe for quinoa yeast bread is a favorite among gluten-free breads because it has a texture and mouth feel similar to whole grain wheat bread. For more dense but delicious yeast bread recipes made with single grains, see *The Ultimate Food Allergy Cookbook and Survival Guide* or *Easy Breadmaking for Special Diets* as described on the last pages of this book. For delicious yeast bread recipes made with grain combinations and several stabilizers in each recipe, see *The Gluten Free Gourmet Bakes Bread* by Bette Hagman.

   Baking for any special diet became much easier in the 1990s with the advent of bread machines. With the right bread machine, you can make wheat-free, gluten-free, or any other special yeast bread much more easily.

Any bread machine can be used on the dough cycle to perform the initial mixing and kneading and the first rise for your bread. Then restart the cycle and allow the dough to knead for another 3 to 5 minutes. Remove the dough from the machine, and stir or knead in additional ingredients such as nuts or raisins by hand if you are using them. Put the dough in a prepared loaf pan, and proceed with the second rise and baking as in the recipes below.

If you use a programmable bread machine on which you can control the length of the last rising time, your machine can do almost the whole job of making yeast bread for you. All you have to do is measure the ingredients into the machine and start the cycle. To find out more about programmable bread machines and how to choose the right type of machine for your special diet, see *Easy Breadmaking for Special Diets* as described on the last pages of this book.

Quinoa Raisin Yeast Bread

This tasty bread has an amazingly wheat-like texture for a gluten-free loaf. Try it toasted for breakfast.

> ¼ cup water
> ⅓ cup apple juice concentrate
> About 4 large or 3 extra large eggs*, or enough to measure
>   ¾ cup in volume, at room temperature
> 2 tablespoons oil
> ¾ teaspoon salt
> 1 teaspoon cinnamon
> 4 teaspoons guar or xanthum gum
> 2½ cups quinoa flour
> ¾ cup tapioca starch
> 2¼ teaspoons active dry yeast
> ½ cup raisins

Heat the water and apple juice concentrate to about 115ºF. Beat the eggs lightly and add them to the other liquids. Stir together the dry ingredients in a large electric mixer bowl. With the mixer running at low speed, gradually add the liquid mixture and oil. Beat the dough for three minutes at medium speed. Scrape the dough from the beaters and the sides of the bowl into the bottom of the bowl. Oil the top of the dough and the sides of the bowl, and cover the bowl with a towel. Put the bowl in a warm (85°F to 90°F) place and let the dough rise for 1 to 1½ hours. Beat the dough again for three minutes at medium speed. Stir in the raisins by hand. Oil and flour an 8 by 4 inch loaf pan. Put the dough in the pan and allow it to rise in a warm place for about 20 to 30 minutes, or until it barely doubles. Preheat the oven to 375°F. Bake the loaf for about 50 to 70 minutes, loosely covering it with foil after the first 15 minutes to prevent excessive browning. Makes one loaf. To make this bread more easily with a bread machine, see "About Yeast Breads" on pages 40 to 41.

   *Note: If you are allergic to eggs, use ¾ cup warm water in their place.

Buckwheat "Rye" Bread

The caraway seeds and rye flavor powder give this bread a rye-like taste.

   ½ cup water
   ¼ cup apple juice concentrate
   About 4 large or 3 extra large eggs*, or enough to measure
      ¾ cup in volume, at room temperature
   3 tablespoons oil
   1¼ teaspoon salt
   1 tablespoon caraway seed (optional)
   ¼ to ½ teaspoon rye flavor powder, to taste (optional)
      (See "Sources," page 82)
   1 tablespoon guar or xanthum gum
   2 cups buckwheat flour
   1¼ cup tapioca starch
   2¼ teaspoons active dry yeast

Heat the water and apple juice concentrate to about 115°F. Beat the eggs lightly and add them to the other liquids. Stir together the dry ingredients in a large electric mixer bowl. With the mixer running at low speed, gradually add the liquid mixture and oil. Beat the dough for three minutes at medium speed. Scrape the dough from the beaters and the sides of the bowl into the bottom of the bowl. It will be very sticky. Oil the top of the dough and the sides of the bowl, and cover the bowl with a towel. Put the bowl in a warm (85°F to 90°F) place and let the dough rise for 1 to 1½ hours. Beat the dough again for three minutes at medium speed. Oil and flour an 8 by 4 inch loaf pan. Put the dough in the pan and allow it to rise in a warm place for about 20 to 35 minutes, or until it barely doubles. Preheat the oven to 375°F. Bake the loaf for about 50 to 65 minutes, loosely covering it with foil after the first 30 to 45 minutes if it is getting excessively brown. Makes one loaf. To make this bread more easily with a bread machine, see "About Yeast Breads" on pages 40 to 41.

*Note: If you are allergic to eggs, use ¾ cup warm water in their place.

Main and Side Dishes

Main and side dishes do not cause as many problems as breads do for people on gluten-free diets. After all, there are plenty of gluten-free meats and vegetables to eat! Therefore, this chapter contains just a few recipes that feature the less common gluten-free grains. The oven grain and oven vegetable recipes on pages 45 to 50 can simplify your life by being part of an oven meal as described on page 12 of this book.

If you are looking for gluten-free Mexican or Italian main dishes, see *The Ultimate Food Allergy Cookbook and Survival Guide* and *Allergy Cooking with Ease* which are described on the last pages of this book.

Quinoa Stuffed Peppers

Because quinoa contains high-quality protein, this is a very satisfying vegetarian main dish. You can substitute 3 cups of any other cooked grain for the quinoa and water if you wish.

1½ cups quinoa
3 cups water
1 pound frozen chopped spinach
2 tablespoons oil
2 teaspoons salt
¾ teaspoon pepper
3 tablespoon chopped fresh or 3 teaspoons dry sweet basil
2 tablespoons paprika (optional - for color)
6 green bell peppers, seeded
Additional oil

Wash the quinoa thoroughly by putting it in a strainer and rinsing it under running water until the water is no longer foamy. Combine it with 3 cups of water in a saucepan. Bring it to a boil, reduce the heat, and simmer it for 15 to 20 minutes. Cook the spinach in the 2 tablespoons of oil, adding no water, for 5 to 10 minutes, or until it is barely tender. Mix the quinoa and spinach with the seasonings and stuff the mixture into the peppers. To cook the peppers in the traditional way, put a little oil into a heavy frying pan, lay the peppers in the pan on their sides, cover the pan, and fry the peppers slowly, turning them to brown all sides, for 30 to 45 minutes. Or, if you would rather bake the peppers, parboil them for 5 minutes before stuffing them, stuff them, and bake them in an oiled casserole dish at 350°F for 45 minutes. Makes 4 to 6 servings.

Oven Grains

This is an easy and delicious way to cook grains. These grains are convenient as part of an oven meal.

Teff: Cooking time: 1 to 1½ hours

> 1 cup teff
> 3 cups water
> 1 tablespoon oil
> ½ teaspoon salt

Quinoa: Cooking time: 1 hour. Quinoa should be thoroughly rinsed in a strainer under running water to remove the soapy coating before cooking it.

> 1 cup quinoa
> 2½ cups water
> 1 tablespoon oil
> ½ teaspoon salt

Millet: Cooking time: 30 to 45 minutes

> 1 cup millet
> 3½ cups water
> 1 tablespoon oil
> ½ teaspoon salt

Sorghum*: Cooking time: 2½ to 3 hours

    1 cup sorghum (milo)
    3½ cups water
    1 tablespoon oil
    ½ teaspoon salt

Brown rice*: Cooking time: 1 to 1½ hours

    1 cup brown rice
    2½ cups water
    1 tablespoon oil
    ½ teaspoon salt

White rice*: Cooking time: 1 to 1¼ hours

    1 cup white rice
    2½ cups water
    1 tablespoon oil
    ½ teaspoon salt

Wild rice*: Cooking time: 1½ to 2 hours

    1 cup wild rice
    4 cups water
    1 tablespoon oil
    ½ teaspoon salt

Oat groats*: Cooking time: 2 hours

    1 cup oat groats
    2¾ cups water
    1 tablespoon oil
    ½ teaspoon salt

Choose one set of ingredients from above or from the previous page. Turn your oven on to 350°F or the temperature needed for other dishes you will be baking with the grain as part of an oven meal.

Combine the grain, water, oil, and salt in a 2 to 3 quart casserole dish. Put the lid on the casserole or cover the dish tightly with foil. Bake until the grain is tender and all the water is absorbed. Approximate baking times are listed with each grain's ingredient list on the preceding pages. Fluff the grain and serve.

The first time you make this recipe with each grain, or if you are using a different oven temperature for other dishes in your oven meal, check the grain near the end of its baking time and add more water if it is beginning to dry out. If you wish to bake a grain for the same amount of time as the entree of an oven meal, the baking time can be extended. The first time you extend the baking time, be sure to check the grain and add water as it bakes. Record how much extra water you add, and the next time you use the longer baking time or a higher temperature, you can add the extra water initially.

Makes 4 to 6 servings.

Notes about sorghum, rice, and oats: Whole-grain sorghum is usually not available at health food stores but can be ordered from Purcell Mountain Foods. See "Sources," page 82. Rice is included in this recipe because some readers may be able to eat it, and the many other gluten-free cookbooks do not include recipes for how to cook rice in the oven to go with your oven meals. Oat groats are included for those whose doctors allow them to eat oats as part of a gluten-free diet.

Oven Root Vegetables or Butternut Squash

These oven vegetables are delicious as well as easy to cook.

White Potatoes

1½ pounds white potatoes
½ teaspoon salt
Dash of black pepper (optional)
2 tablespoons oil

Sweet Potatoes

2 pounds regular (orange) or white sweet potatoes
¼ teaspoon salt
2 tablespoons oil

Turnips

2 pounds turnips
¼ teaspoon salt
2 tablespoons oil

Butternut Squash

2½ pounds butternut squash
¼ teaspoon salt
2 tablespoons oil

Choose one set of ingredients from the preceding page or above. Peel the vegetables and cut them in half lengthwise. Seed the squash. Slice the vegetables into ¼ inch slices. For variety, you may wish to cut the white potatoes into ¾ inch cubes or leave them unpeeled. Put the slices or cubes into an 11 inch by 7 inch baking dish, sprinkle them with the seasoning(s), and drizzle the oil over them. Stir them to coat all of the slices or cubes with the oil.

Turn your oven on to 400°F for cubed white potatoes or to 350°F for sliced white potatoes or any of the other vegetables. Bake cubed white potatoes for 45 minutes to one hour without turning them. Bake sliced white potatoes or the other vegetables for 1½ to 2 hours, turning the slices after the first hour. Makes 4 to 6 servings.

Oven Carrots, Cabbage, or Cauliflower

When you try this recipe, you will find that oven-baked carrots are the sweetest, most delicious vegetables you have ever tasted.

Carrots

2 to 2½ pounds carrots
½ cup water*
½ teaspoon salt
2 tablespoons oil

Cabbage

1 head of cabbage (about 1½ to 1¾ pounds)
½ teaspoon salt
¼ teaspoon ground black pepper (optional)
½ cup water
3 tablespoons oil

Cauliflower

1 head of cauliflower (about 1½ to 1¾ pounds)
½ teaspoon salt
¼ teaspoon ground black pepper (optional)
½ cup water
3 tablespoons oil

Choose one set of ingredients from above. If you are using the carrots, peel them and cut them in half lengthwise, or cut them into quarters if they are large. Lay the carrot sticks parallel to each other in a 2 to 3 quart glass casserole dish. If you are wish to use pre-peeled mini-carrots, see the end of this recipe for special directions. If you are using the cabbage, coarsely shred it and put it into a 3 quart glass casserole dish. If you are using the cauliflower, cut it into very small florets and dice the core. Put it into a 3 quart glass casserole dish. Add the seasoning(s) and water to the casserole dish and drizzle the oil over the top of the vegetables. Cover the dish with its lid or cover it tightly with foil. Bake at 350°F for 1 to 1½ hours. Makes 4 to 6 servings.

*Note on pre-peeled mini-carrots: Pre-peeled carrots absorb a lot of water in the peeling process so they don't caramelize well in this recipe, and you will not need to use any water with them. Bake them without water, salt, or oil for one hour. Drain off the water that accumulates in the casserole. Add the salt and oil and bake for another hour or more until they dry out and begin to caramelize.

Oven Beans or Peas

Using frozen vegetables makes this recipe a snap!

> 2 10-ounce packages frozen lima beans, cut green beans,
>   or peas OR 1¼ pounds of fresh cut green beans or
>   shelled peas
> ⅔ cup water
> ¼ teaspoon salt
> 2 tablespoons oil

Stir together all of the ingredients in a 2 to 3 quart glass casserole dish. Cover the dish with its lid or cover it tightly with foil. Bake at 350°F for 1 to 1½ hours for the beans or 1 hour for the peas. Makes 4 servings.

Millet "Mashed Potatoes"

> 1 cup whole millet
> 4½ cups water
> ½ teaspoon salt, or to taste

Put the millet in a strainer and rinse it with cold water. Combine the millet with the water and salt in a saucepan. Bring it to a boil, reduce the heat, and simmer for 35 minutes. Remove the pan from the heat and beat the millet with a spoon until it is smooth. Makes 4 to 6 servings.

Polenta

2 cups finely ground cornmeal for polenta (not regular cornmeal)
4 cups water
1½ teaspoons salt, or to taste
Oil OR spaghetti sauce or pesto and cheese (optional)

In a small bowl, stir together the cornmeal and 2 cups of cold water. Put the remaining 2 cups of water and the salt in a large saucepan and bring it to a boil. Add the wet cornmeal to the boiling water a little at a time, stirring the mush constantly. Return to a boil; then reduce the heat to a low simmer and cook it over very low heat for 1 hour. Stir the mush thoroughly every five minutes while it is cooking. It will be very stiff when it is done.

For an Italian dinner, spread the cornmeal mush on a platter and top it with pesto or spaghetti sauce and cheese. Serve it with extra sauce and cheese. For spaghetti sauce and pesto recipes see *The Ultimate Food Allergy Cookbook and Survival Guide, Allergy Cooking with Ease,* or *Easy Cooking for Special Diets* as described on the last pages of this book.

To serve the polenta for breakfast as scrapple, pack the cooked mush into an oiled loaf pan and refrigerate it overnight or until it is very firm. Turn the mush out of the pan and slice it about ½ inch thick. Put a tablespoon or two of oil into a small skillet and heat it for about a minute over medium to medium high heat. Put the mush slices in the skillet a few slices at a time and cook them until they are brown on one side. Then turn them and cook until the other side is brown.

Makes 4 to 6 servings

Desserts

Desserts are a part of many of life's important moments – birthdays, holidays, graduations, and family celebrations of many kinds. You want to have a dessert worthy of the occasion and the company to set on your table on these special days. Using the recipes in this chapter, you can make a dessert that is delicious and that everyone – even those on gluten-free diets – can enjoy.

Gluten-free baked goods tend to be fragile, and this is more of a problem for large goods, such as cakes and pies, than it is for small items such as muffins and crackers. However, there are ways around this problem. When you make a cake, oil and flour the pan(s) and then line them with parchment paper or waxed paper to make the layers easier to remove from the pan(s). If you bake your cake in an attractive ceramic baking pan rather than a metal tin, you can serve it directly from the pan even for very special occasions.

Gluten-free pie crusts are too fragile to roll out, but there is also a way around this problem. Make the pie crust as directed in the recipe on page 57 and divide the dough in half. Press half of it on to the bottom and sides of your pie dish. Add the filling. Crumble the rest of the dough over the top of the filling and bake. Homemade pie is so delicious that no one will complain about it having a crumb topping rather than a rolled top crust.

For more pie fillings (cherry, grape, peach, and more), fruit cobblers, ice cream, sorbet, and many other gluten-free desserts, see *The Ultimate Food Allergy Cookbook and Survival Guide* and *Allergy Cooking with Ease* which are described on the last pages of this book.

Also, take note of the especially simple desserts in this chapter such as "Easy Fruit Crumble," page 53, "Grain-Free Easy Fruit Crumble," page 54, and "Easy Fruit Tapioca," page 64. These can be made quickly and easily, so make them often and turn any day into a special occasion!

Easy Fruit Crumble

This recipe is as easy to make as it is delicious. Although millet flakes are currently unavailable in the United States, perhaps the rising number of people on gluten-free diets will convince an entrepreneur or company to bring them back, or maybe you have a British friend who will send you some. If your doctor allows you to eat oats, this dessert is great made with oatmeal.

> 4 cups fresh blueberries or peeled and sliced apples or peaches
>   OR 4 cups drained water-packed canned peaches
>   OR 1 pound frozen blueberries
> ¾ to 1 cup date sugar, divided
> ¼ cup arrowroot or tapioca starch
> 2 to 6 tablespoons water, divided
> 1 cup millet flakes or oatmeal, uncooked
> 1 teaspoon cinnamon
> ¼ cup oil

Preheat your oven to 325°F. Taste the fruit you are going to use. If it is sweet, use ¼ cup date sugar with the fruit. If it is tart, use ½ cup date sugar with the fruit. Combine the ¼ or ½ cup date sugar and the arrowroot or tapioca starch and stir them into the fruit in an 8 inch square baking dish. If you are using fresh fruit, sprinkle 4 tablespoons water over the blueberries or apples. Sprinkle 2 tablespoons water over fresh peaches or frozen blueberries. No water is needed with canned peaches.

In a small bowl, combine the cereal, remaining ½ cup date sugar, and cinnamon. Stir in the oil until the mixture is crumbly. Stir in 2 tablespoons of water. Sprinkle the mixture on top of the fruit. Bake for 30 to 40 minutes or until the topping browns and the fruit is tender when pierced with a fork. Makes 6 to 8 servings.

No-Grain Easy Fruit Crumble

This is my favorite dessert with its pairing of sumptuous fruit and a crunchy topping.

4 cups fresh blueberries or peeled and sliced apples or peaches
    OR 4 cups drained water-packed canned peaches
    OR 1 pound frozen blueberries
¼ cup arrowroot or tapioca starch
½ to ¾ cup date sugar, divided
Up to 4 tablespoons water
¼ cup almond meal/flour
⅔ cup unsweetened coconut
⅓ cup chopped or sliced almonds
Cinnamon – 1¼ teaspoon with the apples, ¼ teaspoon
    with the other fruit
¼ cup oil

Preheat your oven to 400°F. Combine the fruit, arrowroot or tapioca starch, 1 teaspoon cinnamon (with the apples only), and ¼ to ½ cup of date sugar (depending on how sweet the fruit is) in a deep 8 or 9 inch square baking dish or 2 to 3-quart casserole dish. Add just enough water to barely moisten the starch and date sugar. The starch-liquid mixture should be like a thick paste. How much water you will need to add will depend on how "juicy" your fruit is; with canned peaches you will not need to add any water.

In a bowl, stir together the remaining ¼ cup date sugar, almond meal, coconut, almonds, and ¼ teaspoon cinnamon. Pour the oil over the mixture and stir until it is evenly distributed. Sprinkle the nut mixture over the fruit in the baking dish. Bake for 10 minutes. Then cover it with foil to prevent excessive browning. Bake for another 30 to 35 minutes or until hot and bubbly. Makes about 6 servings.

Apple Pie

You will never miss the sugar in this all-time favorite pie.

⅞ cup apple juice concentrate, possibly divided
6 to 7 apples, peeled, cored, and sliced (about 5 cups of slices)
1 teaspoon cinnamon
2 tablespoons tapioca starch or arrowroot OR 3 tablespoons
    quick-cooking tapioca
1 baked single pie crust OR 1 batch of pastry for a two-crust pie,
    pages 57 to 58

If you are using the quick-cooking tapioca, allow it to soak in the ⅞ cup apple juice in a saucepan for 5 minutes. Then add the apples and cinnamon to the pan, bring it to a boil, and simmer until the apples are tender. If you are using the tapioca starch or arrowroot, cook the apples with ⅝ cup of the juice and the cinnamon until tender. Stir the starch into the remaining ¼ cup of the juice and stir the mixture into the apples. Cook over medium heat until it is thick.

For a one-crust pie, cool the apple filling for 10 minutes, then pour it into a cooled, baked pie crust and refrigerate the pie.

For a two-crust pie, preheat your oven to 400°F. You do not need to simmer the apples until they are tender. If you are using the tapioca, just bring the apple-tapioca mixture to a boil and put it into the crust. If you are using the tapioca starch or arrowroot, bring the apples plus ⅝ cup apple juice and cinnamon to a boil, stir in the starch mixture, and simmer until it is thickened before putting the filling into the crust. Bake your 2-crust pie for 10 minutes at 400°F. Then turn down the oven temperature to 350°F and bake it for 40 to 50 minutes more, or until the bottom crust of the pie begins to brown. Makes 1 pie, or about 6 servings.

Blueberry Pie

This pie is delicious and very easy to make using frozen fruit.

¾ cup apple juice concentrate, thawed
2 tablespoons arrowroot or tapioca starch
1 16-ounce package frozen unsweetened blueberries
1 baked single pie crust OR 1 batch of pastry for a two-crust pie,
    pages 57 to 58

Stir together the juice and arrowroot or tapioca in a saucepan. Add the blueberries and cook the mixture over medium heat until it thickens and boils, stirring it frequently. For a one-crust pie, cool the filling for 10 minutes, put it into a cooled, baked pie crust, and refrigerate the pie. For a two-crust pie, preheat your oven to 400°F. Put the filling into the crust and bake the pie for 10 minutes at 400°F. Then turn down the oven temperature to 350°F and bake it for about 30 to 40 minutes more or until the bottom crust of the pie begins to brown. Makes 1 pie, or about 6 servings.

Brown Sugar Pumpkin Pie

This pie is too delicious to serve only on holidays.

1 envelope unflavored gelatin
1 cup water
1 16-ounce can pumpkin
1 cup date sugar OR ¾ to 1 cup brown sugar, to taste
1 teaspoon cinnamon
1 teaspoon nutmeg
¼ teaspoon ground cloves
¼ teaspoon allspice
¼ teaspoon ginger
1 baked pie crust, pages 57 to 58

Put the water in a saucepan and sprinkle the gelatin over it. Bring it to a boil and heat it over medium heat until the gelatin is dissolved. Add the pumpkin, date sugar or brown sugar, and spices and stir until the filling is thoroughly mixed. Pour it into the cooled baked pie crust and refrigerate the pie until firm. Makes 1 pie, or about 6 servings.

Traditional Pie Crust

Teff

3 cups teff flour
½ teaspoon salt
½ cup oil
5 to 6 tablespoons water

Buckwheat

3 cups buckwheat flour
½ teaspoon salt
¾ cup oil
6 to 8 tablespoons water

Amaranth

1½ cups amaranth flour
¾ cup arrowroot
½ teaspoon salt (optional)
½ cup oil
¼ cup water

Oat

3 cups oat flour
½ teaspoon salt (optional)
½ cup oil
¼ cup water

Choose one set of ingredients from the previous page. In a large bowl, combine the flour(s) with the salt. Add the oil and blend it in thoroughly with a pastry cutter. Add the water and mix the dough until it begins to stick together, adding an extra 1 to 2 teaspoons of water if necessary. Divide the dough in half. Preheat your oven to 400°F. For one-crust pies, press each half of the dough into a glass pie dish, gently prick it with a fork, and bake it until the bottom of the crust begins to brown. The baking times for each kind of crust are as follows:

Teff: 15 to 18 minutes
Buckwheat: 15 to 18 minutes
Amaranth: 15 to 18 minutes
Oat: 15 to 20 minutes at

For a two-crust pie, press half of the dough into the bottom of a glass pie dish. Fill the crust with the filling of your choice. Crumble the second half of the dough and sprinkle it over the filling. Bake as directed in the filling recipe. This recipe makes two single pie crusts or an ample amount of pastry for a two-crust pie.

Coconut Pie Crust

Although unusual, this pie crust is delicious and goes especially well with pumpkin filling. It is best made with very finely shredded coconut.

2 cups very finely shredded or shredded unsweetened coconut
    (See "Sources," page 80 for very finely shredded coconut).
Melted coconut oil – ⅜ cup with very finely shredded coconut
    OR ¼ cup with regular shredded coconut

Preheat your oven to 300°F. Thoroughly mix the coconut with the melted coconut oil and press it onto the bottom and sides of a glass pie dish. Bake the crust for 12 to 15 minutes, or until it begins to brown. Cool the crust completely and fill it with the pumpkin filling recipe on page 56 or the fruit pie filling of your choice on pages 55 to 56. When using a fruit pie filling, cook it until it is thickened and the fruit is tender. Allow the filling to cool slightly before putting it into the crust. Makes one single pie crust.

Sorghum Spice Cake

Don't slow your family down on finishing this cake up soon after you bake it. It's best fresh and tends to become dry with storage.

2 cups sorghum (milo) flour
½ cup date sugar
2½ teaspoons baking powder
1 teaspoon cinnamon
¼ teaspoon cloves
¼ teaspoon allspice
1½ cups pureed or thoroughly mashed bananas
⅜ cup oil

Preheat your oven to 375°F. Oil and flour an 8 or 9 inch round or square cake pan. Thoroughly mash or puree the bananas. If the date sugar contains hard lumps, press it through a sieve with the back of the spoon to get rid of the lumps. Stir together the flour, date sugar, baking powder, and spices in a large bowl. In a separate bowl or cup, combine the pureed bananas and oil. Stir the liquid ingredients into the dry ingredients until they are just mixed in. Put the batter into the prepared baking pan. Bake the cake for 25 to 30 minutes or until a toothpick inserted into the center of the cake comes out dry. Cool the cake thoroughly before frosting it with "Date Frosting," page 60. Serve the cake from the pan. Makes one 8 inch or 9 inch one-layer cake

Date Frosting

⅔ cup water
1½ tablespoon sorghum (milo) flour
1 cup date sugar

Remove any lumps in the date sugar by pressing it through a wire mesh strainer with the back of a spoon. Mix the water and flour in a small saucepan. Cook the mixture over medium heat until it is thick, smooth, and bubbly, stirring frequently. Remove the pan from the heat, add the date sugar, and beat the frosting with a spoon until it is smooth. Frost the cake immediately. Makes enough frosting for one 8 or 9 inch cake.

Gingerbread

This is great served from the baking pan with whipped cream.

1¼ cups quinoa flour
½ cup tapioca starch
2½ teaspoons baking powder
¾ teaspoon ginger
1 teaspoon cinnamon
¾ cup molasses
¼ cup water
¼ cup oil

Preheat your oven to 350°F. Oil and flour an 8 or 9 inch square cake pan. Combine the flours, baking powder, and spices in a large bowl. Mix the molasses with the water until the molasses is "dissolved." Then add the oil and mix thoroughly. Stir the liquid ingredients into the dry ingredients until they are just combined. Put the batter into the prepared baking pan. Bake the cake for 30 to 35 minutes, or until a toothpick inserted in its center comes out dry. Makes one cake, or about 9 servings.

Carob Cake

The quinoa flour makes this cake as satisfying as it is delicious.

1½ cups quinoa flour
¾ cup tapioca starch
⅓ cup carob powder
1½ teaspoons baking soda
1 cup apple juice concentrate, thawed
½ cup oil

Preheat your oven to 350°F. Oil and flour an 8 or 9 inch round or square cake pan. If you wish to remove the cake from the pan for serving, also line the pan with waxed or parchment paper. Combine the flours, carob powder, and baking soda in a large bowl. Mix the juice and oil and stir them into the dry ingredients until they are just mixed in. Put the batter into the prepared pan and bake the cake for 25 to 30 minutes or until a toothpick inserted in its center comes out dry. Cool it in the pan for 10 minutes and then remove it from the pan if you wish to, or serve the cake from the pan. When the cake is completely cool, frost it with homemade buttercream icing or "German Chocolate Frosting," below. This recipe may be doubled to make a two-layer cake.

"German Chocolate" Frosting

¾ cup maple syrup OR ⅜ cup honey
1 cup finely shredded unsweetened coconut
1 cup finely chopped nuts

Boil the maple syrup down to ⅜ cup volume (it will reach ⅜ cup about the time it starts to foam) or warm the honey. Add the coconut and nuts while it is still hot, mix it well, and spread it on the cake immediately. This recipe makes enough frosting for one 8 or 9 inch cake and may be doubled for a two-layer cake.

Chocolate Cake

This cake is so light and has such a great chocolate flavor that you will forget it's gluten-free. The tasters of this recipe said it ranged from not sweet enough to too sweet, so I settled on a "medium" amount of sugar. Feel free to adjust the amount of sugar if you prefer it more or less sweet.

    8 large eggs
    ½ cup sugar
    ½ cup potato starch
    ½ cup cocoa
    ¼ cup water
    2 teaspoons baking powder

Preheat your oven to 350°F. Oil and flour two 8 or 9 inch square or round cake pans. Separate the eggs; if you have two* glass measuring cups, put the whites and yolks into two different cups. The volume of the whites should be 1 cup minus 1 tablespoon. The volume of the yolks should be ½ cup plus 1 tablespoon. If the volumes are off by more than one tablespoon, adjust the volume as follows: If the volume is high, remove some white or yolk. If it is low, break another egg and add white or yolk to the respective cup to bring the volume up to the required level.

Beat the egg whites on high with an electric mixer until frothy. Then add the sugar about 1 tablespoon at a time with about 30 seconds between additions as the egg whites are beating. Beat until stiff peaks form. Then either set the bowl aside, or if your mixer only has one bowl, scrape the beaten egg whites into another large bowl. It is not necessary to wash the bowl or beater before using them to make the rest of this recipe.

Beat the egg yolks on medium with an electric mixer. Add the potato starch and beat until smooth. Add the cocoa and water alternately, beating until smooth. Scrape down the sides of the bowl and beat the whole mixture for two minutes. Add the baking powder and beat for one minute more, scraping down the sides of the bowl after about 30 seconds (in the middle of the minute of beating after adding the baking powder).

Pour the chocolate mixture into the egg whites. Fold the two mixtures together quickly; do not overmix. Pour the batter into the prepared pans. Bake for 30 to 35 minutes or until a toothpick inserted into the center of the deepest layer comes out dry. Cool the cake layers on racks for 10 minutes and then remove them from the pans. When the cake is completely cool, frost it with homemade butter-cream icing, a double batch of "German Chocolate Frosting," page 61, "Chocolate Glaze," below, or serve it with whipped cream. Makes about 12 servings.

*Note on measuring egg whites and yolks: If you have only one measuring cup for liquids, measure and correct the volume of the egg whites first. If the whites become contaminated with the yolks, they will not beat properly. However, it is alright to contaminate the yolks with a little egg white. If you measure the whites first, you can re-use the cup for the yolks without washing it between the two ingredients.

Chocolate Glaze

6 ounces (about 1 cup) chocolate chips
¼ cup heavy cream

Combine the chocolate chips and cream in the top of a double boiler over simmering water. Heat and stir them until the chips are melted and they are thoroughly mixed with the cream. Or, to make this topping in a microwave oven, put the chips and cream into a glass bowl. Heat them together in a microwave oven on 50% power, stirring every 30 seconds, until the chips are melted and uniformly mixed into the cream. Drizzle and spread the chocolate mixture over the cake. Makes enough to "frost" one layer or drizzle over two layers of cake.

Easy Fruit Tapioca

This makes a great dessert for an oven meal and can go into the oven along with your other dishes without preheating the oven first.

1 16- to 20-ounce can of juice-packed sliced peaches, pears, or
   pineapple chunks, not drained, OR water-packed pie cherries,
   drained
¼ cup minute tapioca
1 cup water or fruit juice with the peaches, pears, or pineapple,
   OR 1 cup apple juice concentrate plus ½ cup water with the
   cherries

In a 1½-quart casserole dish, combine all of the ingredients. Bake uncovered at 350°F for 40 to 60 minutes or until the tapioca is clear. Makes 4 servings.

Baked Apples or Pears

4 large baking apples or pears
½ cup apple juice concentrate, apple juice, or water
½ teaspoon cinnamon (optional)

Core the fruit and put it in a 2½-quart glass casserole dish with a lid. Pour in the juice or water and sprinkle the cinnamon down the center of the fruit. There is no need to preheat the oven for this dessert. Bake at 350°F for 40 to 50 minutes or longer for the apples or 1 to 1½ hours for the pears, or until the fruit is tender when pierced with a fork. The exact baking time is not crucial so this is good dessert to have as part of an oven meal. Makes 4 servings.

Cookies, the Sanity Savers

Cookies can be lifesavers and sanity savers, especially for mothers of young children. Because most of the cookies in this chapter are fruit sweetened, they make healthy snacks for the young and old alike. They relieve those feelings of deprivation you may have on a special diet and therefore are as good for your soul as they are for your body.

There are three chocolate chip cookie recipes in this chapter. While gluten is not found in pure chocolate, it can be present in other components of chocolate bars and chocolate chips. Look at your health food store for chocolate chips which are gluten-free to use in your homemade cookies. Enjoy Life™ makes very good gluten-, soy-, and dairy-free chocolate chips. They are small and have a very intense chocolate flavor, so they "go farther" in cookies, and you may wish to use the smaller amount of chocolate chips listed in these recipes.

As in the rest of this book, the recipes in this chapter are just a sampling of the types of cookies you can have on a gluten-free diet. For more recipes, including recipes for easy drop cookies made with all of the gluten-free flours, see *The Ultimate Food Allergy Cookbook and Survival Guide* which is described on the last pages of this book.

Chocolate Brownies

These chewy brownies are the favorite of my gluten-intolerant friend Connie Tysdal.

> 2 1-ounce squares unsweetened chocolate
> ⅜ cup oil
> 1 cup sugar
> 2 large eggs
> ½ teaspoon salt
> ¾ cup buckwheat flour
> ½ teaspoon baking powder

Preheat your oven to 350°F. Oil an 8-inch square metal baking pan. Line the bottom and two opposite sides of the pan with an 8-inch wide strip of parchment or waxed paper. Also oil the paper. Melt the chocolate in a double boiler over boiling water or carefully microwave it in a glass bowl, stirring often, until it is just melted. Stir the oil into the melted chocolate thoroughly. Add the sugar, eggs, and salt and stir thoroughly. In a separate bowl, stir together the flour and baking powder. Add the dry ingredients to the chocolate mixture and stir until just mixed. Spread the batter in the prepared pan. Bake for 30 minutes or until the top has a dull crust and a toothpick inserted into the brownies comes out with just a few moist crumbs on it. Cool in the pan. Then cut into squares. Makes 16 brownies.

Cakey Corn Brownies: If you prefer more cake-like brownies rather than chewy brownies, substitute ¾ cup corn flour for the buckwheat flour and decrease the amount of oil used to ⅓ cup.

Carob Brownies

These cookies are a delicious and satisfying favorite for those who must avoid all grains.

> 1 cup amaranth flour
> ¼ cup arrowroot
> ⅓ cup carob powder
> ½ teaspoon baking soda
> ¾ cup apple juice concentrate, thawed
> ¼ cup oil

Preheat your oven to 350°F. Oil and flour a 9 inch by 5 inch metal loaf pan. If your carob powder contains lumps, press it through a strainer with the back of a spoon to remove the lumps before measuring it. Combine the amaranth flour, arrowroot, carob powder, and baking soda in a bowl. In another bowl or measuring cup, stir together the apple juice concentrate and oil. Stir the liquid ingredients into the dry ingredients until just mixed and immediately put the batter into the prepared pan. Bake for 20 minutes. The batter will puff up during baking and then collapse either near the end of the baking time or after you remove the brownies from the oven. Do not overbake. The "toothpick test" does not apply to these brownies; if you test them with a toothpick, the toothpick will come out with wet dough on it. These brownies have a moist, chewy texture. Makes 8 to 10 brownies.

Amaranth Biscotti

These cookies are a gluten-free variation of my favorite cookies that my aunt made for Christmas every year.

2 cups amaranth flour
1 cup arrowroot
1½ teaspoon baking powder
¼ teaspoon salt (optional)
½ cup sliced almonds
¾ cup Fruit Sweet™
⅓ cup oil
1 teaspoon natural almond flavor
1 teaspoon natural vanilla flavor

Preheat your oven to 350°F. Stir together the flours, salt, baking powder, and almonds in a large bowl. In a small bowl, mix the Fruit Sweet™, oil, and flavorings; then stir them into the dry ingredients. Put the dough on a lightly oiled baking sheet, and use your hands to form it into a flat-topped loaf about 14 inches long, 3 inches wide, and 1 inch tall. Bake it at 350°F for 25 to 30 minutes, or until it is set and is barely beginning to brown. Remove it from the oven and, using a serrated knife, cut it down the middle lengthwise and slice it cross-wise into ¾ to 1 inch slices. Lay the slices down on their cut sides on the cookie sheet. Bake the slices and additional 15 to 20 minutes, or until they are hard and lightly browned. Makes 2½ dozen cookies.

Quinoa Almond Cookies

This cookie has several different "personalities" depending on what you use for the sweetener. Try all the varieties – they're delicious in different ways.

1½ cups quinoa flour
2¼ teaspoons baking powder
½ cup almond meal/flour
¼ cup sliced almonds (optional)
½ cup oil
½ teaspoon almond flavoring
½ cup honey (for crisp cookies) OR ½ cup honey plus
    ½ cup water (for soft cookies) OR 1 cup apple juice
    concentrate, thawed (for fruit-sweetened soft cookies)

Preheat your oven to 375°. Combine the flour, baking powder, almond meal, and almonds in a large bowl. Thoroughly mix the oil with the honey, honey and water, or juice in a small bowl, and then immediately pour it into the dry ingredients. Stir the dough until it is just mixed. Drop it by teaspoonfuls onto an ungreased baking sheet. For the crisp cookies, flatten the cookies with an oiled glass bottom or your fingers held together. Bake the cookies at 375°F for 7 to 10 minutes. Makes about 2 dozen crisp or 3 dozen soft cookies.

Very crisp and flaky variation: Make the "crisp cookie" variation of this recipe using ½ cup honey for the sweetener and also decrease the flour to 1 cup. You will not need to flatten the cookies with your fingers or a glass because the batter will be much thinner and will spread readily. Place the cookies at least 3 to 4 inches apart on the baking sheet. Bake as above.

Fig Bars

These cookies will remind you of Fig Newtons™.

Filling:

    8 ounces dried figs
    1 cup water
    2 teaspoons natural vanilla flavoring (optional)

Dough:

    3 cups amaranth flour
    1 cup arrowroot
    ¾ cup oil
    ⅜ cup to ½ cup cold water

To make the filling, remove the stems from the figs. Combine the figs and water in a saucepan, bring them to a boil, reduce the heat, and simmer them on low heat for 30 minutes. Cool the figs, stir in the optional vanilla, and puree them in a blender or food processor until they are smooth. While the filling is cooking, make the dough.

Mix together the amaranth flour, arrowroot, and oil with a pastry cutter until the mixture is crumbly. Gradually add enough of the water to make a soft dough. Divide the dough in half and flatten each half unto a small square.

Preheat your oven to 400°F. Roll one half of the dough out into an 8 by 12 inch rectangle on an ungreased cookie sheet and spread it with the filling. Roll the other half of the dough out into an 8 by 12 inch rectangle on a well-floured pastry cloth or roll it out between two pieces of waxed or parchment paper and peel off the top piece. Invert the pastry cloth or waxed or parchment paper with the dough on it onto the top of the fig filling and dough on the baking sheet. Peel off the pasty cloth or paper from the dough. Bake for 25 to 30 minutes or until it begins to brown. Cool for 10 minutes, then carefully cut it into 1½ inch squares with a sharp knife. Makes about 3 dozen cookies.

Carob Wafers or
Sandwich Cookies

You can put these sandwich cookies together with sugar-free jam or carob chips or eat them plain, as "Carob Wafers," for everyday use. For a special occasion, fill the sandwiches with white fondant and they will remind you of Oreos™.

1½ cups carob powder
1½ cups tapioca starch or arrowroot
3 teaspoons baking powder
1 cup apple juice concentrate
½ cup oil
About ⅔ cup all-fruit (sugarless) jam or jelly
     OR 1 cup carob chips (optional)

Preheat your oven to 350ºF. Combine the carob powder, tapioca starch, and baking powder in a large bowl. Mix together the juice and oil and stir them into the dry ingredients until they are thoroughly mixed in. Roll the dough into 1 inch balls and place them on an ungreased baking sheet. Flatten each ball to ⅛ to ¼ inch thickness with an oiled glass bottom or your fingers held together. Bake the cookies for 10 to 12 minutes or until they feel set when you touch them. Remove them from the baking sheet with a spatula and cool them completely. If you are using the carob chips, melt them in the top of a double boiler over water that is just below the boiling point, stirring them frequently. As soon as they are melted, remove the top of the double boiler from the pan. Or microwave the carob chips, stirring often, until melted. Put the cookies together in pairs, with their bottoms together, using the melted carob chips, jelly or jam. Makes about 2 dozen sandwich cookies or 4 dozen plain carob wafers.

"Oreos™" variation: See *Allergy Cooking with Ease* or a general purpose or candy cookbook for a white fondant recipe which can be used to put these cookies together in pairs to make sandwich cookies that will remind you of Oreos™.

Quinoa Carrot Cookies

These are as nutritious as they are delicious since they are made with quinoa flour (which is high in protein and calcium) and carrots (a great source of vitamin A).

>2 cups quinoa flour
>⅔ cup tapioca starch or arrowroot
>2½ teaspoons baking powder
>1 teaspoon cinnamon
>⅞ cups apple juice concentrate, thawed
>⅓ cup oil
>1½ cups grated carrots
>½ cup raisins (optional)

Preheat your oven to 350°F. Oil your baking sheets. Mix together the flours, baking powder, and cinnamon in a large bowl. Stir in the raisins. Combine the juice, oil, and carrots and stir them into the flour mixture until they are just mixed in. Drop the batter by heaping teaspoonfuls onto an ungreased cookie sheet and, if you like flat rather than round cookies, flatten the balls of dough with your fingers. Bake for 12 to 15 minutes or until the cookies begin to brown on the bottom. Makes 2 to 3 dozen cookies.

Teff Shortbread

These are my gluten-intolerant friend Joan Hinkemeyer's favorite cookies.

>2 cups teff flour
>1½ teaspoons baking powder
>½ cup oil
>¼ cup Fruit Sweet™
>1 large egg plus enough water to bring its volume up to
>   ¼ cup

Preheat your oven to 350°F. Stir together the flour and baking powder. Break the egg into a measuring cup and beat it slightly with a fork. Add water to the cup to bring the volume up to ¼ cup. Then stir the Fruit Sweet™ and oil into the egg mixture. Add the liquid ingredients to the dry ingredients, mixing with a spoon and your hands until the dough sticks together. If the dough is too dry to stick together, add 1 to 2 tablespoons of water. Turn the dough out onto a baking sheet. Using a rolling pin, roll the dough out to ¼ inch thickness. Cut the dough into 1 by 3 inch bars with a sharp knife. Bake the cookies for 15 to 20 minutes until they are set and beginning to brown. Cut the cookies again on the same lines after you remove them from the oven. Remove the cookies from the baking sheet with a spatula. Put them on paper towels to cool completely. Makes 2 to 3 dozen cookies.

Amaranth Shortbread

1¼ cups amaranth flour
1 cup arrowroot
½ teaspoon baking soda
⅜ cup oil
½ cup pineapple juice concentrate, thawed

Preheat your oven to 350°F. Combine the amaranth flour, arrowroot, and baking soda in a large bowl. Stir together the oil and juice and add them to the dry ingredients, mixing with a spoon and your hands until the dough sticks together. If necessary, add 1 to 2 tablespoons of water to help the dough come together. Roll the dough out to ¼ inch thickness on an ungreased baking sheet and cut it into 1 by 2 to 3 inch rectangular bars. Bake for about 15 to 20 minutes or until the cookies begin to brown. Cut the cookies again on the same lines, if necessary, after you remove them from the oven. Remove the cookies from the baking sheet with a spatula. Put them on paper towels to cool completely. Makes 2½ to 3 dozen bars.

Pizzelles

These traditional Italian Christmas cookies can be made with or without the anise flavoring. You can use them as ice cream cones if you leave out the flavoring and roll them into cone shapes as soon as you remove them from the iron.

1½ cups quinoa flour
½ cup tapioca flour
½ teaspoon baking soda
½ cup melted butter or coconut oil or other (liquid) oil
½ cup apple juice concentrate, thawed
1½ teaspoons anise flavoring (optional)

Begin heating the iron. Brush the plates with the oil you are using to make your pizzelles. Combine the flours and baking soda in a large electric mixer bowl. In a small bowl, stir together the oil, juice, and flavoring (if used), and pour them into the dry ingredients. Beat the dough on low speed until the flour is all moistened, then beat it on medium speed for one minute. If you are using a type of oil other than coconut oil or butter, brush both the top and the bottom of the iron with oil before cooking each cookie. Put one heaping tablespoon of dough in the iron. (You may need more – this is a starting point as you determine how much dough you should put in to fill the iron when you close it). Cook each cookie for 20 to 30 seconds, or until it is golden brown, and remove it from the iron using two forks. (You may have to experiment to determine what cooking time makes the cones easiest to remove). Lay them flat on paper towels to cool. Makes about 2 to 3 dozen 6-inch pizzelles or about 15 pizzelles which are 8-inch circles that break apart into quarter-circles.

Ice cream cones variation: Use a pizzelle iron that makes medium-sized cookies, or if you have a krumkake iron, that is ideal. Immediately after removing each cookie from the iron, roll it into a cone shape. If you wish to have perfectly shaped cones, roll them around metal cone-shaped forms and allow them to cool completely before removing the forms. Makes 1 to 1½ dozen cones.

Carob Pizzelles

We always had anise-flavored pizzelles when I was a young child, but in my teens, chocolate pizzelles became popular, so we had both for Christmas. This recipe is a take-off on chocolate pizzelles.

1 cup quinoa flour
½ cup carob powder
½ cup tapioca flour
½ teaspoon baking soda
½ cup melted butter or coconut oil or other (liquid) oil
1 cup apple juice concentrate, thawed

Begin heating the iron. Brush the plates with the oil you are using to make your pizzelles. Combine the flours, carob powder, and baking soda in a large electric mixer bowl. In a small bowl, stir together the oil and juice, and pour them into the dry ingredients. Beat the dough on low speed until the flour is all moistened, then beat it on medium speed for one minute. If you are using a type of oil other than coconut oil or butter, brush both the top and the bottom of the iron with oil before cooking each cookie. Put one heaping tablespoon of dough in the iron. (You may need more – this is a starting point as you determine how much dough you should put in to fill the iron when you close it). Cook each cookie for 20 to 30 seconds, or until it is beginning to brown, and remove it from the iron using two forks. (You may have to experiment to determine what cooking time makes the cones easiest to remove). Lay them flat on paper towels to cool. Makes about 3 dozen 6-inch pizzelles or about 18 pizzelles which are 8-inch circles that break apart into quarter-circles.

Carob ice cream cones variation: Use a pizzelle iron that makes medium-sized cookies, or if you have a krumkake iron, that is ideal. Immediately after removing each cookie from the iron, roll it into a cone shape. If you wish to have perfectly shaped cones, roll them around metal cone-shaped forms and allow them to cool completely before removing the forms. Makes about 1½ dozen cones.

Oatmeal Raisin Cookies

These cookies are fragile but delicious and are an excellent source of fiber. They are included in this book for those whose doctors allow oats on a gluten-free diet.

2 cups white raisins
2 cups white grape juice
½ cup oil
2 cups oat flour
2 cups oatmeal
1 teaspoon baking soda
1½ teaspoons cinnamon
1 cup brown raisins
½ cup chopped nuts (optional)

Soak the white raisins in the grape juice overnight. In the morning, puree them using a hand blender or in a blender or food processor. Add the oil and blend again briefly. Preheat your oven to 375°F. Combine the oat flour, oatmeal, baking soda, cinnamon, brown raisins, and nuts in a mixing bowl. Add the raisin puree and stir until it is just mixed into the flour mixture. Drop the batter by heaping teaspoonfuls onto an ungreased baking sheet and bake for 15 to 18 minutes, or until the cookies are lightly browned. Makes about 6 dozen cookies.

Quinoa Drop Cookies or Chocolate Chip Cookies

2 cups quinoa flour
⅔ cup tapioca starch
2½ teaspoons baking powder
⅞ cup Fruit Sweet™
⅓ cup oil
¾ to 1 cup chocolate or carob chips, raisins, or chopped
    nuts (optional)

Preheat your oven to 350ºF. Combine the flours and baking powder in a large bowl. Stir together the Fruit Sweet™ and oil. Then stir the liquid ingredients into the dry ingredients until they are just mixed in. Quickly fold in the optional raisins, nuts or chips. Drop the batter by heaping teaspoonfuls onto an ungreased baking sheet. Bake for 10 to 15 minutes, or until the cookies begin to brown. Makes about 2½ dozen cookies.

Corn Drop Cookies or Chocolate Chip Cookies

Although fragile, these cookies have a wonderful flavor. Eat them fresh when they are soft and moist!

    1½ cups corn flour
    ½ cup tapioca starch
    ¼ teaspoon salt
    2 teaspoons baking powder
    2 large eggs
    ½ cup oil
    ½ cup honey
    ½ to ¾ cup chocolate or carob chips, raisins, or chopped
        nuts (optional)

Preheat your oven to 375ºF. Oil the baking sheets. Combine the flour, starch, salt, and baking powder in a large bowl. Lightly beat the eggs. Add the honey and oil to the eggs and mix them together thoroughly. Then stir the liquid ingredients into the dry ingredients until they are just mixed. Quickly fold in the optional raisins, nuts or chips. Drop the batter by heaping teaspoonfuls onto an ungreased baking sheet. Bake for 7 to 10 minutes, or until the cookies begin to brown. Makes about 2 dozen 3 inch cookies.

Double Chocolate Chip Cookies

You get double chocolate in these cookies – chocolate batter and chocolate chips.

> ¾ cup non-hydrogenated trans-fat-free shortening such as
> Spectrum Naturals™ brand (See "Sources," page 82).
> 1¼ cups brown sugar
> 2 ounces (2 squares) unsweetened baking chocolate
> 2 large eggs
> 2 teaspoons vanilla
> 2¾ cups buckwheat flour
> ½ teaspoon baking powder
> ¾ teaspoon baking soda
> ¼ teaspoon salt
> ¾ to 1 cup chocolate chips (optional)

In a double boiler or microwave oven, carefully heat and stir the chocolate until it is just melted. Allow it to cool. With an electric mixer, cream the shortening and sugar. Add the melted chocolate, eggs and vanilla and beat until smooth and creamy. Stir together the flour, baking powder, baking soda and salt. Gradually add them to the creamed mixture while beating on medium speed. The dough will be stiff. Stir in the chocolate chips. Refrigerate the dough one hour or longer.

Preheat your oven to 375°F. Roll the dough into 1-inch balls and place them at least 2 inches apart on an ungreased baking sheet. Bake for 10 to 13 minutes or until the cookies just begin to brown on the bottom. Makes about 4 dozen cookies.

References and Internet Resources

Dumke, Nicolette M. *Allergy Cooking with Ease.* Adapt Books, Allergy Adapt, Inc., 1877 Polk Avenue, Louisville, CO 80027, Original edition (Starburst Publishers), 1992; Revised edition, 2007.

Dumke, Nicolette M. *Easy Breadmaking for Special Diets.* Adapt Books, Allergy Adapt, Inc., 1877 Polk Avenue, Louisville, CO 80027, 1995; Revised edition, 2007.

Dumke, Nicolette M. *Easy Cooking for Special Diets: How to Cook for Weight Loss/Blood Sugar Control, Food Allergy, Heart Healthy, Diabetic and "Just Healthy" Diets – Even if You've Never Cooked Before.* Adapt Books, Allergy Adapt, Inc., 1877 Polk Avenue, Louisville, CO 80027, 2007.

Dumke, Nicolette M. *The Ultimate Food Allergy Cookbook and Survival Guide.* Adapt Books, Allergy Adapt, Inc., 1877 Polk Avenue, Louisville, CO 80027, 2007.

Gottschall, Elaine. *Breaking the Vicious Cycle: Intestinal Health through Diet.* Kirkton Press, Ontario, Canada, Revised edition, 1994.

Hagman, Bette. *The Gluten-Free Gourmet: Living Well Without Wheat.* Henry Holt, New York, Revised edition, 2000.

Hagman, Bette. *The Gluten-Free Gourmet Bakes Bread.* Henry Holt, New York, 1999.

www.celiac.com

www.food-allergy.org

www. gluten.net

Sources of Special Foods and Products

This is a listing of the manufacturers of some of the special foods and products used in the recipes in this book which are not readily available in certain areas. It includes mail-order and Internet sources of these products. Your health food store can order foods from these sources, or your can order directly from many of them yourself.

ALMOND MEAL/FLOUR:

Bob's Red Mill Natural Foods, Inc.
5209 S.E. International Way
Milwaukie, OR 97222
(503) 654-3215
(800) 349-2173
www.bobsredmill.com

BAKING POWDER, GLUTEN-FREE:

Bob's Red Mill Baking Powder
Bob's Red Mill Natural Foods, Inc.
5209 S.E. International Way
Milwaukie, OR 97222
(503) 654-3215
(800) 349-2173
www.bobsredmill.com

Featherweight Baking Powder (corn and sodium-free)
The Hain Celestial Group, Inc.
4600 Sleepytime Drive
Boulder, CO 80301
(800) 434-4246
www.hain-celestial.com

CHOCOLATE CHIPS, DAIRY, SOY AND GLUTEN-FREE:

Enjoy Life™ Semi-Sweet Chocolate Chips
Enjoy Life™ Natural Brands, LLC
3810 N. River Road
Schiller Park, IL 60176
888-50-ENJOY
www.enjoylifenb.com

COCONUT, FINELY SHREDDED, UNSWEETENED:

Jerry's Nut House, Inc.
2101 Humboldt Street
Denver, CO 80205
(303) 861-2262

FLOUR , GRAINS, AND GRAIN PRODUCTS:

Almond meal/flour, amaranth, arrowroot, buckwheat, carob, corn, fava, garbanzo, garfava, millet, oat, potato flour and starch, quinoa, sorghum, teff, and other gluten-free flours, starches, and baking mixes:

Bob's Red Mill Natural Foods, Inc.
5209 S.E. International Way
Milwaukie, OR 97222
(503) 654-3215
(800) 349-2173
www.bobsredmill.com

Buckwheat, corn, millet, oat, and more:

Arrowhead Mills
The Hain Celestial Group, Inc.
4600 Sleepytime Drive
Boulder, CO 80301
(800) 434-4246
www.hain-celestial.com

Buckwheat and Bean Pasta:

Eden Foods, Inc.
701 Tecumseh Road
Clinton, MI 49236
(517) 456-7424
(888) 424-EDEN (3336)
www.edenfoods.com

Quinoa Flour and Gluten-free Pasta:

The Quinoa Corporation
Post Office Box 279
Gardena, CA. 90248
(310) 217-8125
www.quinoa.net

Rice Bread, Rice Pasta, and other items:

Ener-G Foods, Inc.
P. O. Box 84487
Seattle, WA 98124
(206) 767-6660
(800) 331-5222
www.ener-g.com

Sorghum, Whole Grain:

Purcell Mountain Farms
HCR 62 Box 284
Moyie Springs, ID 83845
(866) 440-2326
www.purcellmountainfarms.com

MEASURING CUPS AND OTHER KITCHEN EQUIPMENT:

King Arthur Flour Baker's Catalogue
P.O. Box 876
Norwich, Vermont 05055
(800) 827-6836
www.kingarthurflour.com

RYE FLAVOR POWDER (GLUTEN-FREE) AND OTHER GLUTEN-FREE FLOURS AND BAKING PRODUCTS:

Authentic Foods
1850 W. 169th Street, Suite B
Gardena, CA 90247
(310) 366-7612
www.authenticfoods.com

SHORTENING, NON-HYDROGENATED, TRANS-FAT FREE:

Spectrum Naturals™ Organic All Vegetable Shortening
Spectrum Organic Products, Inc.
5341 Old Redwood Highway, Suite 400
Petaluma, CA 94954
www.spectrumorganics.com

SWEETENERS:

Date Sugar
NOW Natural Foods *(order through your health food store)*
395 S. Glen Ellyn Road
Bloomingdale, IL 60108
(800) 283-3500
www.nowfoods.com

Fruit Sweet™, Grape Sweet™, Pear Sweet™
Wax Orchards, Inc.
P.O. Box 25448
Seattle, WA 98665
(800) 634-6132
www.waxorchards.com

THICKENERS/BINDERS:

Guar and Xanthum Gums
Bob's Red Mill Natural Foods, Inc.
5209 S.E. International Way
Milwaukie, OR 97222
(503) 654-3215
(800) 349-2173
www.bobsredmill.com

YEAST, ACTIVE DRY, GLUTEN-FREE:

Bob's Red Mill Natural Foods, Inc.
5209 S.E. International Way
Milwaukie, OR 97222
(503) 654-3215
(800) 349-2173
www.bobsredmill.com

Active dry and quick-rise, corn, gluten- and preservative-free:

Red Star Yeast and SAF Yeast
Universal Foods Corporation
Consumer Service Center
433 E. Michigan Street
Milwaukee, WI 53202
(414) 271-6755
www.redstaryeast.com

The Red Star Yeast company is a great information source but does not sell direct to consumers. To purchase Red Star™ or SAF™ yeast in 1 or 2-pound bags, contact:

King Arthur Flour Baker's Catalogue
P.O. Box 876
Norwich, Vermont 05055
(800) 827-6836
www.kingarthurflour.com

About Measurements

You may occasionally need to measure "unusual" amounts like ⅜ cup or ⅛ teaspoon. The easiest and most accurate way to do this is to have a liquid measuring cup with ⅛ cup markings, a set of dry measuring cups that contains a ⅛ cup measure, and a set of measuring spoons that has a ⅛ teaspoon. You can order such kitchen equipment from the King Arthur Flour Baker's Catalogue (See "Sources," page 82) but in the meantime, use this table to make your recipes work.

⅛ teaspoon	= ½ of your ¼ teaspoon measure	
⅜ teaspoon	= ¼ teaspoon + ⅛ teaspoon	
⅝ teaspoon	= ½ teaspoon + ⅛ teaspoon	
¾ teaspoon	= ½ teaspoon + ¼ teaspoon	
⅞ teaspoon	= ½ teaspoon + ¼ teaspoon + ⅛ teaspoon	
1 teaspoon	= ⅓ tablespoon	= ⅙ fluid ounce
1½ teaspoons	= ½ tablespoon	= ¼ fluid ounce
3 teaspoons	= 1 tablespoon	= ½ fluid ounce
½ tablespoon	= 1½ teaspoons	= ¼ fluid ounce
1 tablespoon	= 3 teaspoons	= ½ fluid ounce
2 tablespoons*	= ⅛ cup	= 1 fluid ounce
4 tablespoons	= ¼ cup	= 2 fluid ounces
5⅓ tablespoons	= ⅓ cup	= 2⅔ fluid ounces
8 tablespoons	= ½ cup	= 4 fluid ounces
16 tablespoons	= 1 cup	= 8 fluid ounces
⅛ cup	= 2 tablespoons*	= 1 fluid ounce
¼ cup	= 4 tablespoons	= 2 fluid ounces
⅜ cup	= ¼ cup + 2 tablespoons*	= 3 fluid ounces
⅝ cup	= ½ cup + 2 tablespoons*	= 5 fluid ounces
¾ cup	= ½ cup + ¼ cup	= 6 fluid ounces
⅞ cup	= ¾ cup + 2 tablespoons*	= 7 fluid ounces
	OR ½ cup + ¼ cup + 2 tablespoons*	
1 cup	= ½ pint	= 8 fluid ounces
1 pint	= 2 cups	= 16 fluid ounces
1 quart	= 4 cups OR 2 pints	= 32 fluid ounces
1 gallon	= 4 quarts	= 128 fluid ounces

It is important to measure accurately in all baking, but it is critical in baking with gluten-free flours. They are much less forgiving than wheat because they lack the structure, due to gluten, that holds "normal" baked goods together and helps them rise. Therefore, please do not take offense at this detailed lesson on measuring accurately.

First of all, be sure to use the right kind of measuring cup for the ingredient you are measuring. Measure dry ingredients with nested cups, sold in sets, which are usually metal or opaque plastic. To measure flour, stir the flour to loosen it. Using a large spoon, lightly spoon it into the cup. Level it off with a straight-edged knife or spatula. To measure flour, salt, baking powder, spices, and other dry ingredients with measuring spoons, dip the spoon into the container, stir up the ingredient to loosen it, and fill the spoon generously. Pull it out and level it off with a straight edged knife or spatula, or level spices using the straight edge of the hole in the spice container.

To measure white sugar, spoon it into the cup (the same type used for flour) and level it off. To measure brown sugar, press it into the cup firmly until it is level with the top edge of the cup.

Measure liquids using glass, pyrex, or clear plastic cups with markings on them. To measure, fill the cup with liquid until the meniscus (the bottom of the curve of the liquid) lines up with the line on the cup. Get down on your knees so you can read the cup at eye level. You can measure more than one liquid ingredient in the same cup by adding them sequentially to the cup. For instance, if you need ½ cup water, ¼ cup thawed apple juice concentrate, and ⅛ cup of oil, do this: Add water to the ½ cup line, add apple juice to the ¾ cup line, and then add oil to the ⅞ cup line. Stir them together right in the measuring cup and add them to the dry ingredients. That saves you having to wash an extra bowl. To measure small amounts of liquids in measuring spoons, fill them until the surface is level. If you let the liquid bead up over the top of the spoon, you'll get more of the liquid than is intended in your recipe.

*Note on the table on the previous page: In my experience, measuring tablespoons are all a little scanty of ¹⁄₁₆ cup, so 2 tablespoons is a little short of ⅛ cup. Therefore, if you need to measure, for example, ⅜ cup of liquid, it will probably be more accurate to "eyeball" an amount halfway between ¼ cup and ½ cup than to use ¼ cup plus two tablespoons.

Index to the Recipes by Grain Used

This index will help you find recipes in this book by the major grain or grain alternative that they contain. The recipes that do not contain a grain or grain alternative are not listed in this index but can be found in the "General Index" on page 89. Arrowroot and tapioca flour are used as binders in many recipes in this book. They are included in the listing below only when they are the main flour-type ingredient in a recipe.

POTATO:

Chocolate Cake	62

QUINOA:

Quinoa Pancakes	25
Quinoa Granola	28
"Graham" Crackers	34
Quinoa Sesame Seed Crackers	36
Quinoa Raisin Yeast Bread	41
Quinoa Stuffed Peppers	44
Oven Grains	45
Gingerbread	60
Carob Cake	61
Quinoa Almond Cookies	68
Quinoa Carrot Cookies	71
Pizzelles	73
Ice Cream Cones	73
Carob Pizzelles	74
Carob Ice Cream Cones	74
Quinoa Drop or Chocolate Chip Cookies	75

RICE (including white rice brown rice, and wild rice):

Oven Grains	45

SORGHUM:

Sorghum Pancakes	24
Sorghum Pineapple Muffins	33
Sorghum Crackers	35
Sorghum Banana Bread	39
Oven Grains	45
Sorghum Spice Cake	59
Date Frosting	60

TAPIOCA:

Almond Waffles	26
Grain-Free Easy Fruit Crumble	54
Apple Pie (filling)	55
Blueberry Pie (filling)	56
Blueberry Pie (filling)	56
Easy Fruit Tapioca	64
Carob Wafers or Sandwich Cookies (like Oreos™)	70

TEFF:

Teff Pancakes	24
Teff Waffles	27
Teff Pineapple Muffins	34
Teff Crackers	36
Oven Grains	45
Pie Crust, Traditional	57
Teff Shortbread	71

General Index

Informational sections appear in italics.
Recipes appear in standard type.

Books to Help You with
Your Special Diet

Gluten-Free Without Rice introduces you to gluten-free grains and grain alternatives other than rice such as teff, millet, sorghum, quinoa, buckwheat, tapioca, arrowroot, corn, potato starch, and more. It gives you over 75 delicious recipes for muffins, crackers, bread, pancakes, waffles, granola, main and side dishes, cookies, and desserts. (Even ice cream cones!)With this book you can cook easily for a gluten-free diet without relying on rice. Whether you have celiac disease or food allergies, this book will make it easier and more enjoyable to stay on your diet and will help you to improve your health.

ISBN 978-1-887624-15-2 . . . . $9.95

The Ultimate Food Allergy Cookbook and Survival Guide: How to Cook with Ease for Food Allergies and Recover Good Health gives you everything you need to survive and recover from food allergies. It contains medical information about the diagnosis of food allergies, health problems that can be caused by food allergies, and your options for treatment. The book includes a rotation diet that is free from common food allergens such as wheat, milk, eggs, corn, soy, yeast, beef, legumes, citrus fruits, potatoes, tomatoes, and more. Instructions are given on how to personalize the standard rotation diet to meet your individual needs and fit your food preferences. It contains 500 recipes that can be used with (or without) the diet. Extensive reference sections include a listing of commercially prepared foods for allergy diets and sources for special foods, services, and products.

ISBN 978-1-887624-08-4 . . . . $24.95

Allergy Cooking With Ease **(Revised Edition)**. This classic all-purpose allergy cookbook was out of print and now is making a comeback in a revised edition. It includes all the old favorite recipes of the first edition plus many new recipes and new foods. It contains over 300 recipes for baked goods, main dishes, soups, salads, vegetables, ethnic dishes, desserts, and more. Informational sections of the book are also totally updated, including the extensive "Sources" section.

ISBN 978-1-887624-10-7 . . . . $19.95

Easy Breadmaking for Special Diets contains over 200 recipes for allergy, heart healthy, low fat, low sodium, yeast-free, controlled carbohydrate, diabetic, celiac, and low calorie diets. It includes recipes for breads of all kinds, bread and tortilla based main dishes, and desserts. Use your bread machine, food processor, mixer, or electric tortilla maker to make the bread YOU need quickly and easily.

Revised Edition – ISBN 978-1-887624-11-4 . . . . $19.95

Original Edition – ISBN 1-887624-02-3 . . . . $14.95

Easy Cooking for Special Diets: How to Cook for Weight Loss/Blood Sugar Control, Food Allergy, Heart Healthy, Diabetic and "Just Healthy" Diets – Even if You've Never Cooked Before. This book contains everything you need to know to stay on your diet plus 265 recipes complete with nutritional analyses and diabetic exchanges. It also includes basics such as how to grocery shop, equip your kitchen, handle food safely, time management, information on nutrition, and sources of special foods.

ISBN 978-1-887624-09-1 . . . . $24.95

The Low Dose Immunotherapy Handbook: Recipes and Lifestyle Tips for Patients on LDA and EPD Treatment gives 80 recipes for patients on low dose immunotherapy treatment for their food allergies. It also includes organizational information to help you get ready for your shots.

ISBN: 978-1-887624-07-7 . . . . $9.95

How to Cope With Food Allergies When You're Short on Time is a booklet of time saving tips and recipes to help you stick to your allergy or gluten-free diet with the least amount of time and effort.

$4.95 or FREE with the order of two other books on these pages

You can order these books on-line by going to www.food-allergy.org or by mail using the order form on the next page.

Mail your order form to:

**Allergy Adapt, Inc.
1877 Polk Avenue
Louisville, CO 80027**

Online orders can also be placed with Amazon.com at www.amazon.com.

Order Form

Ship to:

Name: _____

Street address: _____

City, State, ZIP code: _____

Phone number (for questions about order): _____

Item	Quantity	Price	Total
Gluten-Free Without Rice		$9.95	
Allergy Cooking with Ease*		$19.95	
The Ultimate Food Allergy Cookbook & Survival Guide*		$24.95	
Easy Breadmaking for Special Diets* – Original Edition Revised Edition		$14.95 $19.95	
Easy Cooking for Special Diets*		$24.95	
The Low Dose Immunotherapy Handbook		$9.95	
How to Cope with Food Allergies When You're Short on Time		$4.95 or **FREE**	
Order any TWO of the first six books above and get *How to Cope* **FREE!**	Subtotal		
	Shipping – See chart on next page		
	Colorado residents add 4.1% sales tax		
	Total		

Shipping:

IF YOU ARE ORDERING JUST ONE BOOK, FOR SHIPPING ADD:
  $4.00 for any one of the four starred (*) books above.
  $2.00 for any one of the first or last two (non-starred) books above.

TO ORDER MORE THAN ONE BOOK, FOR SHIPPING ADD:
  $6.00 for up to three starred* and two non-starred books
  $9.00 for four starred* and up to three non-starred books

Call 303-666-8253 if you have questions about shipping calculations or large quantity orders.

Mail this order form and your check to:

Allergy Adapt, Inc.
1877 Polk Avenue
Louisville, CO 80027

Thanks for your order!

Order Form

Ship to:

Name: _____

Street address: _____

City, State, ZIP code: _____

Phone number (for questions about order): _____

Item	Quantity	Price	Total
Gluten-Free Without Rice		$9.95	
Allergy Cooking with Ease*		$19.95	
The Ultimate Food Allergy Cookbook & Survival Guide*		$24.95	
Easy Breadmaking for Special Diets* – Original Edition Revised Edition		$14.95 $19.95	
Easy Cooking for Special Diets*		$24.95	
The Low Dose Immunotherapy Handbook		$9.95	
How to Cope with Food Allergies When You're Short on Time		$4.95 or **FREE**	
Order any TWO of the first six books above and get *How to Cope* **FREE!**	Subtotal		
	Shipping – See chart on page 97		
	Colorado residents add 4.1% sales tax		
	Total		

CPSIA information can be obtained at www.ICGtesting.com
Printed in the USA
LVOW011524051011

249155LV00009B/16/A